THE GOSPEL

OF

THE TWELVE APOSTLES

THE GOSPEL

OF

THE TWELVE APOSTLES

TOGETHER WITH

THE APOCALYPSES

OF

EACH ONE OF THEM

EDITED

FROM THE SYRIAC MS.

WITH A TRANSLATION AND INTRODUCTION

BY

J. RENDEL HARRIS, M.A.

(D. LITT. Dubl.)

FELLOW OF CLARE COLLEGE

WIPF & STOCK · Eugene, Oregon

Wipf and Stock Publishers
199 W 8th Ave, Suite 3
Eugene, OR 97401

The Gospel of the Twelve Apostles
Together with the Apocalypses of Each One of Them,
Edited from the Syriac MS. with a Translation and Introduction
By Harris, J. Rendell
ISBN 13: 978-1-60608-351-2
Publication date 12/04/2008
Previously published by Cambridge University Press, 1900

PREFACE.

THE series of tracts contained in the following pages, from which a selection has already appeared in the *Contemporary Review* for December, 1899, may seem to some to be of too small importance to be honoured with a further publication; but the matter contained in them is new, the Syriac appears to be original rather than, as is so often the case, translated, and the historical situations, which can clearly be made out, have a value of their own in the record of the decline of Eastern Christianity.

My especial thanks are due to Prof. Nestle of Maulbronn, whose acute criticisms and careful proof-reading have added much to the accuracy of the volume.

J. RENDEL HARRIS.

INTRODUCTION.

THE MS. from which the text in this volume is taken is numbered 85 in my private collection (Cod. Syr. Harris 85). In the form in which it reached me it consisted of a pile of damaged and ill-arranged leaves, out of which by much pains I have reconstructed, as far as possible, the order of the book of which they formed a part.

The handwriting is a fine Estrangelo, which I should, apart from the internal evidence, have attributed to the eighth century, at the latest, and as we shall see by and bye that there is internal evidence for bringing the time of the composition of parts, at least, of the volume, down into the seventh or perhaps the eighth century, it is extremely probable that the ancestry of the book is not a long one, and it is even conceivable that it is altogether without genealogy, and is the copy produced by him who first threw together the matters of which the volume treats.

The volume itself might be described in some such way as Lagarde denotes one of his collections as *Reliquiae Iuris Ecclesiastici*, with which work of Lagarde it has much in common, as we shall see from the detailed table of contents. It is of Jacobite, or West Syrian origin, as may be seen from certain anti-Nestorian extracts taken from the writings of the Patriarch Severus; nor should we be likely to have erred seriously, if we were to describe it as an Edessan document; for, although the colophon of the book is lost, and the earliest pages are also missing, the frequency and prominence with which writings attributed to Jacob of Edessa, and to his friend and correspondent John the Stylite, occur, as well as the extracts taken from the Edessan Doctrine of Addai etc. will probably convince us that the volume was produced in the neighbourhood of Edessa. As Jacob of Edessa died in A.D. 708, the extracts which our MS. gives from his works must be almost, if not quite, contemporary. We shall, therefore, say tentatively that the MS. before us is an Edessan volume of the middle of the eighth century, and if subsequent examination gives us a closer determination of time and place, we may be sure that it will not be one that diverges widely from what we have suggested as probable.

The extent and contents of the volume are as follows:

quires ܐ and ܒ are lost,

quires ܓ to ܗ are intact, and are quinions,—they occupy ff. 1—50 of the MS.,

quire ܘ is imperfect after the first eight leaves, which occupy ff. 51—58,

and from this point on there are numerous lacunae in the MS. There is no quire mark again until the fifteenth (ܝܗ) which apparently occupies ff. 84 onward. There are therefore six quires to be accounted for, more or less completely by the 25 leaves which remain, from which it is clear that a great part of the middle of the MS. is gone.

Now as to the actual contents. They are as follows:

Fol. 1. The questions of Addai the priest to Jacob of Edessa (see Lagarde, *Reliquiae juris ecclesiastici* p. ܡܘ). Our text begins on p. ܩܡܓ, l. 25 of Lagarde, and follows Lagarde until his text breaks off, near the end of Jacob of Edessa's reply to the 71st question of Addai, after which the text continues to the end of the 129th question and answer, so that it appears that Lagarde's text of these questions is not much more than the half of the extant matter. Nor is this all, for there follows another series of questions addressed to Jacob, which clearly belong to the same collection; viz.

fol. 34. Questions of the priest Thomas to Jacob, with the answers of the latter. This series ends on f. 37 recto; and then comes, on

fol. 37 v, another series addressed to Jacob by John the Stylite. This is followed on

fol. 44 v by a series of short chapters, containing replies of the holy fathers to questions which had been sent to them by the Orientals (ܡܕܢܚܝܐ). They end at the top of f. 47 recto, and are immediately followed on fol. 47 r by the Gospel of the Twelve Apostles; with which is incorporated,

fol. 51 v, the Revelation of Simeon Kepha; and on

fol. 53 r, the Revelation of James the Apostle; and on

fol. 54 r, the Revelation of John the little, the brother of James, and they [two] are the sons of Zabdai. This Apocalypse ends on fol. 58 r.

Fol. 58 r contains an extract from the Teaching of Addai, as it was spoken in the city of Edessa. As the text varies a good deal from that published by Phillips, I give the two side by side for purpose of comparison.

Cod. Harris   ed. Phillips (p. ܩܒ)

[Syriac text in two columns]

It will be seen that the divergence between the two texts here quoted is very decided, and it seems natural to conclude that the Doctrine of Addai is here present in a distinct and perhaps an earlier recension. The same extract will be found in Cureton, *Ancient Syriac Documents* pp. 108 and ܠܒ, very nearly as in our MS.

Fol. 58 r. The extract from the Doctrine of Addai is followed by an extract on the Origin of the Nestorian heresy taken from the thirty-eighth discourse of Severus against Grammaticus.

After this leaf there is a lacuna in the MS., and when the text resumes after the lacuna, caused by the loss of an unknown number of leaves, we are in the Apostolic Canons (Lagarde, *Reliquiae* p. ܩܣܗ).

Fol. 59 r, l. 4. Canon of Matthew.

l. 21. Canon of Paul.

Fol. 59 v, l. 6. Canon of Paul and Peter.

After this the MS. is again *in lacuna*. It resumes on fol. 60 r with the conclusion of the Apostolic Canons by the hand of Clement, and then

Fol. 60 r, l. 11. The Canons of Nicaea: some pages are again missing.

Fol. 62 v. End of Canons of Nicaea; commencement of Synod of Ancyra.

Fol. 67 v. Canons of the Synod of Neocaesarea.

Fol. 69 r. Canons of the Synod of Gangra.

Fol. 72 v. Canons of the Synod of Antioch *in encaeniis*.

After some more gaps, we are on f. 77 r in the Canons of the Synod of Laodicea.

Fol. 77 r, l. 13. Canon 20 of Laodicea.

Fol. 83 r, l. 22. A Canon of the Synod of Ephesus.

Fol. 83 v, l. 13. Canons of Chalcedon: a leaf being missing which was apparently the last leaf of the 14th quire, since the next leaf has the quire-mark 15.

Fol. 89 v. End of Canons of Chalcedon.

l. 2. A Canon of Simeon Cananaeus.

l. 18. Questions addressed to Timothy the patriarch of Alexandria.

Fol. 91 v, l. 18. A libellum (ܠܝܒܠܐ) for those who return

from any kind of heresy. After which the MS. is *in lacuna.*

Fol. 92 r, l. 14. On the signification of the names of the heavenly powers.

Fol. 92 v. An extract apparently dealing with the fact that certain names in the O. T. are interchangeable, as that the bird which is called ܚܘܦܐ in the Greek Psalter [cf. Ps. ciii. 17] is called ܟܘܣܝܐ in the prophet Zechariah [cf. Zech. v. 9],

and here the codex abruptly ends.

We have now described, to the best of our ability, the re-arranged mass of leaves. It will be clear from the description that a large part of the original MS. is missing, but that, imperfect as it is, it furnishes a good deal of unedited matter, especially in regard to the questions of Jacob and Addai, imperfectly published by Lagarde, and the Gospel and Apocalypses with which this volume is especially concerned.

The title of the Gospel contained in our MS. is one that naturally attracts the attention of the investigator and of the church historian. For, as is well known, there is a tradition that a Gospel of this name was current in the second century, and fragments, supposed to belong to it, are actually in existence. The tradition comes from Origen and Epiphanius, of whom the former, in his first Homily on Luke, speaks of a Gospel inscribed with the title 'of the twelve Apostles,' and the latter[1], in treating of the Gospels current amongst the Gnostic Ebionites, produces fragments[2] from a Gnostic Gospel according to Matthew, which the Gnostics who use it call ἑβραικὸν, in which fragments Matthew is the spokesman for the rest of the Apostles, so that it has naturally been suggested[3] that the title of the book quoted by Epiphanius was εὐαγγέλιον τῶν ιβ′ ἀποστόλων διὰ Ματθαίου.

The Gospel of the Twelve Apostles.

Now it is not necessary for us to discuss over again the various questions which have arisen with regard to these Gnostic Gospels. What we have to decide is the relation which subsists between our Gospel which has turned up in Syriac and the Gospel from which Epiphanius quotes. Is there any connexion between them, or are

---

[1] *Haer.* 30. 13.

[2] The passages will be found collected in Hilgenfeld, *Nov. Test. extra Canon.*

[3] Harnack, *Geschichte der altchr. Litteratur* I. 208.

they the same ? The Syriac writer has certainly led us to expect
something ancient, for he affirms that the work which he is going
to transcribe has been done out of Hebrew into Greek and out of
Greek into Syriac. This certainly looks as if it was meant that
we had here an original Hebrew Gospel of the Twelve Apostles,
such as we find traces of in Epiphanius.

However, according to the same Epiphanius, the beginning of
the book was as follows:

Ἐγένετο ἐν ταῖς ἡμέραις Ἡρώδου τοῦ βασιλέως τῆς Ἰουδαίας,
ἐπὶ ἀρχιερέως Καϊάφα, ἦλθέ τις Ἰωάννης ὀνόματι, ὃς ἐλέγετο
εἶναι ἐκ γένους Ἀαρὼν τοῦ ἱερέως, παῖς Ζαχαρίου καὶ
Ἐλισάβετ, βαπτίζων βάπτισμα μετανοίας ἐν τῷ Ἰορδάνῃ
ποταμῷ· καὶ ἐξῆλθον πρὸς αὐτὸν Φαρισαῖοι κτέ.

It is not necessary to quote further, for a comparison with the
Syriac text shows that there is no common matter between them.
In the Syriac Gospel John the Baptist does not appear at all, and
although the opening sentences might lead one to expect a
reference to the Baptist, no such reference is made. We are
indeed told, in language that recalls the opening verses of Mark,
that this is

The beginning of the Gospel of Jesus the Christ, the Son of
the living God, according as it is said by the Holy Spirit,

I send an angel before his face, who shall prepare his way:
but no intimation is given as to the person who is denoted by the
angel.

It seems, then, at first sight as if we were in a position to
conclude that there was no point of contact between our Syriac
Gospel and the lost Gospel of the Twelve Apostles: for the former
does not agree in its opening with the latter. It might be added
further that there is hardly anything in the Syriac text which
betrays the twelve Apostles as engaged in its composition. The
twelve do not speak for themselves, nor does Matthew speak for
them. With one slight exception, to be discussed presently, all is
impersonal in the narrative, and any other title would, at first
sight, seem to suit the composition as well as the one which
actually occurs. Unless, then, there is reason to believe that the
evangelical matter has been excerpted from an early Gospel of the
Twelve Apostles, we should have to conclude that the title was
artificial, and in all probability the composition itself late. Such
a conclusion would be in harmony with what we find to be true

of the associated documents with which the Syriac Gospel is connected, and to which it serves as a prologue, for, as we shall presently see, all of the three Apocalypses which follow are eighth century documents, written at some critical point in the history of the Moslem invasion.

On the other hand, we must be careful not to draw too rapid conclusions, for these very Apocalypses are, as is the custom with such documents, reproductions and imitations of earlier works; and if this be so with regard to the Apocalypses, why may it not also be true that the Syriac Gospel of the Twelve may have absorbed or reproduced the language and ideas of an earlier Gospel? In that case it would be more likely that the lost Gospel of the Twelve had been drawn upon than any other work.

We shall admit, however, as a result of a comparison with the extracts from Epiphanius, that the Syriac Gospel cannot be the lost Gospel of the Twelve, even if we reserve our judgment as to the possible use, by excerpts or imitation, of such a lost Gospel by the Syriac writer.

In what sense, then, does the title Gospel of the Twelve Apostles apply to the Syriac work? Is it, as at first sight appears, a purely arbitrary title? Short as the document is, the twelve Apostles have a decided place in it. Their names are given, and not only their names but their tribes, which shows that an attempt has been made to send an Apostle to each tribe. The only difficulty is that James and John, the sons of Zabdai, are said to belong to the same tribe; on the other hand, Andrew is of a different tribe to Peter, which confirms our suspicion that an attempt has been made to find a parallel between the twelve Apostles and the twelve tribes of Israel; and lest we should have any doubt on the matter, the writer goes on to say, that these are the twelve 'disciples to whom he promised twelve thrones *that they might judge Israel.*' Obviously the idea is that the judgment is tribal, and that each Apostle judges a tribe (cf. Luke xxii. 30). And this agrees with the extract from the lost Gospel of Matthew which Hilgenfeld prints from Epiphanius *Haer.* 30. 13, considering it to be the same work as the Gospel of the Twelve, according to which Jesus says to his disciples, 'you, therefore, I wish to be twelve apostles, for the *testimony of Israel.*'

There is, then, a prominence given to the Twelve in the Syriac work, which is sufficient to explain the title, and which finds a

parallel in a passage which has been referred, with some probability, to the lost Gospel of the Twelve.

Moreover, although it is true, as we stated above, that the
Syriac document is almost entirely impersonal, there is one
striking instance to the contrary. We are told that 'Our Lord
commanded them and said to them that they should go out and
evangelize in the four quarters of the world; and *we* carried out
the preaching, lo! from the ends of the earth to the ends of the
same[1].'   Here, then, is a striking instance of the intrusion of the
personal element in the narration, which is sufficient to show that
in the mind of the writer, the composition was really a Gospel of
the twelve Apostles, and to suggest that there is an element
which is definitely parallel to the language of the text quoted by
Epiphanius that 'there was a certain man named Jesus, about
thirty years of age, *who chose us.*'

Let us, then, reserve our judgment as to whether the Syriac
text is an excerpt from or an adaptation of an earlier lost Gospel:
for it may very well be so : if there is as yet no conclusive reason
in favour of such a hypothesis, there is no conclusive reason
against it.

But if we are not able to speak positively with regard to the
use in the Syriac Gospel of the Twelve of a prior Gospel of the
same name, we are able to indicate a group of Syriac writings
with which the new Gospel has much in common.

According to our text the time of Christ's birth is indicated in
the following manner;

"In the 309th year of Alexander the son of Philip the
Macedonian, in the reign of Tiberius (sic) Caesar, in the government of Herod the ruler of the Jews, the angel Gabriel went
down to Nazareth."

The date is peculiar, but it is not original with our writer; for
we are told by Dionysius Bar Salibi that 'Jacob of Edessa, whom
we follow[2], says that our Lord was born in the 309th year of the
Greeks.' We may take it, then, that the reckoning given in our
MS. was the approved Edessan reckoning at the time of the
production of the volume.

Nor is the date an isolated phenomenon, belonging merely
to Jacob of Edessa. If we turn to the Syriac *Doctrine of the*

---

[1] Reading ܟܬܘܪܒܐ ܘܝܣܡ, without the points.

[2] ܕܗܘ ܐܟ ܣܡ ܥܠܝܣ

Apostles[1] we find the dating of the great Day of Pentecost given as follows:

"In the three hundred and thirty-ninth year of the kingdom of the Greeks, in the month Ḥeziran, on the fourth day of the same, which is the first day of the week, and the completion of Pentecost etc."

This document is important, on account of the survival in it of the early belief that the Ascension took place on Sunday and that it coincided with Pentecost, as well as for other early traditions contained in it with regard to the Day of Pentecost. Now its date, 339 of the Greeks, is clearly arrived at by taking the birth of Christ in 309, adding the thirty years of his life, the last of which is the single year[2] of his public ministry, according to the early belief of the Church. Thus the chronology of the Syriac *Doctrine of the Apostles* is the same as that of the Syriac *Gospel of the Apostles*, and it has the appearance of being an early chronology. For one of the MSS. from which the *Doctrine* is published is as early as the fifth or sixth century. It is not, therefore, a reckoning invented by Jacob of Edessa.

That it is a well-established reckoning at Edessa may also be seen in the following way.

In the Martyrdom of Barsamya, bishop of Edessa[3], we have, at the close of the Acts of the Martyrdom, the ecclesiastical genealogy of the saint. His orders are traced back to Simon Peter, who is said to have received the priesthood, along with the rest of the disciples, 'on the Sunday of the Ascension of our Lord to his glorious Father, which is the fourth day of Ḥeziran, which is the nineteenth year of Tiberius Caesar, in the consulate of Rufus and Rubelinus, which year is the year three hundred and forty-one: *for in the year three hundred and nine was the manifestation of our Saviour in the world, according to the testimony which we have found in a correct volume of the archives, which errs not at all in whatever it declares.*' The archives in question are

---

[1] Cureton, *Ancient Syriac Documents*, p. 24.

[2] As soon as the ministry was extended to three or four years, the date of the birth was pushed back, or the date of the passion pushed forward. Thus the Book of the Bee says, "In the 307th year of Alexander the son of Philip...the archangel Gabriel appeared to Mary etc."; and Dionysius Bar Salibi in the passage already quoted says that Eusebius placed the incarnation in the 312th year of the Greeks.

[3] Cureton, *Ancient Syriac Documents*, p. ܒܚ.

clearly the archives of Edessa : and the reckoning is the early
Edessan chronology. But when we examine the Syriac Doctrine
of the Apostles more closely, we find that it is not limited in its
coincidence with the Gospel of the Twelve to a mere matter of
chronology.

In the Doctrine the disciples go to the upper room at Jerusalem
and begin to enquire one of another how they shall preach the
gospel to the world. They are perplexed as to how 'they should
preach his Gospel to strange tongues which they knew not,' and
before 'strange peoples whose tongues we know not.' When
the Day of Pentecost is come and the gift of the Spirit is received,
then 'according to the tongue which each one of them had
received, so he prepared himself to go into the country in which
that tongue was spoken and understood.' It will be seen that the
motive is the same as in the Syriac Gospel, where, in answer to
the prayers of the disciples, there is given 'to each one of them
a tongue and grace, and so Simeon spake with them in Hebrew,
James in Latin' and so on.

Thus there is a common tradition as to the Day of Pentecost,
and a common interpretation as to the gift of tongues in the two
writings.

But if the Syriac Gospel betrays signs of an Edessan origin
when it is compared with the Syriac Doctrine, a much more
striking literary parallel will be found when the Gospel and
attached Apocalypses are compared with another early Syriac
document, known as the *Testament of our Lord.*

The story of this Testament is as follows :

When our Lord had been raised from the dead and had
appeared to his disciples and satisfied them that he was really
risen, they are seized with great fear and they fall upon their
faces. The Lord lays his hand on each of them and raises them
up, and reassures them by promising them the gift of the Holy
Spirit. The Apostles begin to ask the signs of the end of the
world and the events that are then to happen. The Lord promises
them the knowledge of the signs, and also undertakes to tell them
who is the Son of Perdition that is to come, the Adversary and
Enemy. Evil rulers are to arise, who are lovers of money, haters
of truth, slayers of their brethren. Signs are to appear in heaven
and on earth. Detailed prophecies are given as to the miseries
that are coming upon the world and the Church. Special descrip-

tions are given, in the manner of the Sibyl, of the evil fortunes that await particular countries, Cappadocia, Lycia and Lycaonia, etc. etc.

The parallels with our Syriac Apocalypses are obvious. The Testament of our Lord is seen to be itself an Apocalypse, employed as the prologue to a collection of Canons; and the Syriac Gospel and Apocalypses occupy the same position with regard to the decrees of the councils which follow it. There is the same literary model for both collections.

Sufficient comparisons have now been drawn to establish our belief that the new work which we are discussing is Edessan in origin, and belongs to a well-defined Apocalyptic tradition and manner. It is, therefore, more than ever unlikely that there is any fact underlying the statement as to the Hebrew origin of the Gospel of the Twelve Apostles as it appears in our text. If there be any truth in the statement, its confirmation must come from within rather than from without.

We pass on to discuss the actual date of the composition as betrayed by its Apocalyptic element.

The first of the Apocalypses is assigned to Simeon Kepha. Its chief characteristic is a lament over the general decay of faith, coupled with allusions to persecution and martyrdom at the hands of bribed judges.

Apocalypse of Simeon Kepha.

Orthodoxy is confined to a minority and is on the point of disappearing from the earth; many of those who bear the name of Christ are false in their allegiance; they talk perversely and *divide our Lord.* Here the allusion is not to primitive Gnostics (as in 1 John iv. 3, πᾶν πνεῦμα ὃ λύει τὸν Ἰησοῦν), but to the Nestorian heresy, which affirmed two natures in Christ. The Nestorians who profess to have a superior knowledge of the Son shall be handed over to tribute and to pillage and to all manner of evils. But these evils will not be confined to the unorthodox section of the Church: ruin and desolation will be everywhere. But at the last there will be an ecclesiastical reunion; the unorthodox shall come back to the ancient faith, and shall believe in the Son according to the primitive tradition. There will be one flock, as in ancient time. Those that call upon the Lord and adore the Paraclete will be saved.

From this Apocalypse we obtain very little that is in the nature of a historical landmark, beyond the strife between the two sections of the Eastern Church. But we catch the report of hostile movements from without, as well as of misgovernment within; only it is not clear whether the destroying, devastating hosts are Romans, Persians, or Moslems. The conclusion is purely Apocalyptic, and at present there are no signs of the fulfilment of the prophecy that the writer has made.

Apocalypse of James.

The second Apocalypse is assigned to James. It is concerned entirely with the fortunes and destinies of Jerusalem. Its destruction at the hand of the Romans is briefly alluded to, as a nemesis for the Crucifixion of Christ. After this there is a brief interval, and the Apocalypse resumes. A new oppressor comes, who kills and destroys until there is not found in the city any except those that wail and weep. One thinks of the war under Hadrian. After this comes an oppressor who dies in war against his enemies. Another ruler comes, who builds in the Holy City splendid sanctuaries and sets up there the sign that overcomes the wicked. On the completion of his building he dies, and a strong but rough ruler arises from his family.

The ruler who builds the splendid house of the Lord must be Constantine the Great. The sign that overcomes is his ensign of the cross. The emperor that precedes him and dies in war is perhaps Licinius, whose final defeat at the hands of Constantine was speedily followed by his imprisonment and execution. The Apocalypse does not take us to a lower date than the reign of Constantius or perhaps Julian, and its predictive element is extremely small. If we had nothing else to decide dates by, except this Apocalypse of James, we should say that the historical element in it terminated before the death of Julian (363 A.D.) and that there was no internal reason for dating it later than the middle of the fourth century.

Apocalypse of John.

When, however, we come to the Apocalypse made to John, we are carried three or four centuries lower down the stream of time. Amongst the figures that can be recognised in the Apocalyptic drama, three are conspicuous: the first of these is described as one of the kings of the north, who subdues all the peoples by the marvellous sign which appeared to him in heaven; and he is to prosper and to be succeeded by a line of Roman kings. It would be strange if any one else were intended than Constantine the Great, who was a leading figure in the previous Apocalypse. The conquering sign seen in heaven is sufficient to establish the identification. The writer goes on to describe the decline of the Roman power, and the rise of the Persian.

The line of Persian kings culminates in a covetous monarch, under whose rule trade and commerce decline almost to extinction, and who is finally murdered by his own son. After his decease the Persian kingdom soon passes away as the writer has assumed the Roman kingdom to have passed.

Now this king is clearly Chosroes the Great, and the parricide is his son Siroes. The story is told by Gibbon as follows:

"Siroes, who gloried in the rank and merit of his mother Sira, had conspired with the malcontents to assert and anticipate the rights of primogeniture. Twenty-two satraps, they called themselves patriots, were tempted by the wealth and honours of a new reign: to the soldiers, the heir of Chosroes promised an increase of pay; to the Christians, the free exercise of their religion; to the captives, liberty and rewards; and to the nation, instant peace and the reduction of taxes. It was determined by the conspirators that Siroes, with the ensigns of royalty, should appear in the camp; and if the enterprise should fail, his escape was contrived to the Imperial Court. But the new monarch was saluted with unanimous acclamations; the flight of Chosroes (yet where could he have fled?) was rudely arrested (A.D. 628, Feb. 25), eighteen sons were massacred before his face, and he was thrown into a dungeon, where he expired on the fifth day.

"The Greeks and modern Persians minutely describe how Chosroes was insulted, and famished and tortured, by the command of an inhuman son, who, so far, surpassed the example of his father: but at the time of his death what tongue could relate the story of the parricide? what eye could penetrate into the *tower of darkness*? According to the faith and mercy of his Christian enemies, he sunk without hope into a still deeper abyss; and it will not be denied that tyrants of every age and sect are the best entitled to such infernal abodes. The glory of the house of Sassan ended with the life of Chosroes: his unnatural son enjoyed only eight months the fruit of his crimes; and in the space of four years the regal title was assumed by nine candidates, who disputed with sword and dagger the fragments of an exhausted monarchy. Every province and each city of Persia was the scene of independence, of discord and of blood, and the state of anarchy prevailed about eight years longer, till the factions were silenced and united under the common yoke of the Arabian Caliphs."

The period of Persian decline has its leading features and incidents very well sketched by our Apocalyptist. He does not write a complete history of Rome and Persia, but he gives us some of the leading features and the principal figures, as they existed in men's minds at the time when he wrote. We might, perhaps, be surprised that he makes no allusion to the temporary revival of the Roman power under Heraclius, but the reason for this probably lies in the fact that, however real the triumph of Heraclius might have seemed to the West, in the East it was meteoric and transitory. The victories were unfruitful, the invasion did not result in more than a temporary occupation. To the Apocalyptist the military movements of Heraclius were little more than artificial reactions, symptoms rather of the decline of Persia than of the recovery of Rome. But if these considerations are insufficient to explain the omission of the figure of Heraclius from the drama, there is still the further explanation, viz. that the writer of the Apocalypse never intended to put all the leading historical figures on his stage. His drama has three acts, as presented to an Eastern mind:

   (i)   the rise and fall of Rome,
         the leading figure is Constantine the Great.
   (ii)   the rise and fall of Persia,
         the leading figure is Chosroes the Great.
   (iii)   the rise and fall of Arabia,
         the leading figure is Mohammed the prophet.

The third figure, indicating the rise of a third kingdom, breaking in pieces the former kingdoms, is a man from the South, 'a warrior and one whom they call a prophet.'

The people whom he leads are described under the figure of the wind that blows from the South; and it is not

                  the sweet south wind
        That breathes upon a bank of roses,

but the scorching blast, under whose influence the flowers fade away, and the grace of the fashion of nature perishes.

That Mohammed and his followers are intended seems to admit of no doubt: the writer almost throws off the Apocalyptic veil and says openly that the invading army are the descendants

of Ishmael, for 'he, even he, is the people of the South.' They
are to bring desolation upon the whole earth, and to gather much
spoil from those whom they subjugate. Each king that rises is to
be stronger than the one that preceded, and they will gather much
gold and hide it in the earth.

And now the writer becomes definitely Apocalyptic, and begins
to calculate the times that will elapse before God brings judg-
ments upon the Moslems, and causes the decline of their empire.
The time is to be a great week and half a great week. The
writer is making calculations after the manner of the book of
Daniel, but what point the reckoning starts from is not clear[1].
A comparison of his language with that of the Apocalyptic portions
of Daniel shows some coincidences; and the historical character of
the narration is to be lowered accordingly. In fact the historical
landmarks have almost disappeared.

If there is any further historical matter, it lies in the following
considerations.

When the writer tells us that Ishmael is to be the father of a
line of twelve princes, we may suspect that he wishes us to reckon
twelve caliphs, for there is reason to believe that this was an
interpretation commonly given to the prophecy concerning Ishmael
in the book of Genesis. If this allusion, then, is historical, rather
than prophetical, we must bring the date of the book a good way
down into the eighth century. We should then be obliged to
explain the factions which he goes on to foretell as preceding the
downfall of Islam as the Abbassid and Omiyyad caliphates, which
contend for the mastery between the years 746 and 750 A.D.
Further than this we cannot go, and all the other allusions are
pure Apocalypse. The strife at the fountain of waters is said to
be predicted by the Sibyl, and is, therefore, borrowed from some
earlier deposit of the Apocalyptic imagination. The descent of
the man from the North (the ruler of the resuscitated Roman
Empire) is suggested by the conflict between the king of the
North and the king of the South in the eleventh chapter of
Daniel. The return of the Southern people to the place from
whence they came out is foretold, but like the previous prophecy,
it has never been fulfilled. It is perhaps based upon Dan. xi. 9,

---

[1] If he means to date from the actual fall of the Persian empire, we have to
start with a date that is approximately A.D. 640, and then taking the great week at
50 years, we are carried down to A.D. 715.

"The king of the south shall come into his kingdom and return to his own land." It is further prophesied that the Moslems will return to Arabia, in possession of great wealth which they had hidden in a place called Diglath. The meaning of the prediction is obscure. Diglath should be the Tigris: and one remembers that amongst the signs of the end in the Moslem eschatology, one of the principal is the finding of immense quantities of gold and silver in the bed of the Euphrates[1]. So that perhaps a similar tradition underlies the Apocalypse.

The rest of the predictions as to the hosts of Islam becoming a pastoral people and learning war no more have not been fulfilled; so that the work ends in Apocalypse, pure and simple, as the New Testament ends, with eyes turned toward the divine glory, and a dream of good things to come. It appears, then, clearly that our writer began as a historian, and turned into a prophet, as is the custom with writers of Apocalypses. The exact point of his transition from the former character to the latter is not quite clear; it cannot, however, be later than A.D. 750, and may perhaps be somewhat earlier.

Now the paleographical evidence is in favour of placing the MS. somewhere about the same date; and the literary evidence as derived from an examination of the writings bound up in the volume along with the Gospel of the Twelve Apostles is in favour of the same date for the volume, since the works of Jacob of Edessa would hardly be much circulated before his death, which took place in A.D. 708. The MS. may, therefore, be safely assigned to the eighth century.

It almost seems, then, as if the time of composition of the book were nearly the same as the time of its transcription: for the Apocalypses contained in it may be as late as 750 A.D., and the MS. itself can hardly be later. We are thus in possession of a text which, as far as the Apocalyptic matter goes, is so near the autograph that it may almost be identified with it.

Biblical and other quotations.

The Biblical passages show a close acquaintance with the text of the Peshito, although the matter is used with a good deal of independence. For example, the closing chapter of Mark is employed freely, including the last twelve verses. But it should be

[1] See Pococke, *Porta Mosis* p. 263. The eleventh sign '*Cumuli auri et argenti ab Euphrate retecti.*' Dictum a Mohammede fertur, *Non instabit hora illa donec retexerit Euphrates montem aureum*; vel referentibus aliis, *thesaurum auri.*

noticed that the writer does not quote Matt. xxviii. 17 exactly as in the Canon, 'They worshipped him, but some doubted,' but makes the explanation necessary to connect with the Thomas-incident in John, that 'there was *one* among them who doubted *concerning the resurrection.*'

Of non-biblical writers the only one that is definitely alluded to is the Sibyl, but which Sibylline oracle is referred to in the allusion to a conflict at a certain fountain of waters, I have not been able to determine. Besides this open allusion to the Sibyl, there is no doubt a great deal of Apocalyptic matter which is common to a cycle of Syriac writers, and which can be paralleled from such texts as the Testament of the Lord Jesus Christ, and as Mr Conybeare suggests to me, the Armenian Seventh Vision of Daniel. *The Sibyl.*

In one passage there appears to be a curious parallel between the *Gospel of the Twelve Apostles* and the Apocryphal *Acts of Thomas.* *The Acts of Thomas.*

When the author of the new Gospel describes the Apostles as praying for illumination in the upper room, he uses language which appears to coincide with the following passage from the sixth act of Thomas (tr. Wright: p. 199):

> "To Thee be glory, Thou that art wakeful from all eternity and the Awaker of men, living and making alive. Thou art God, the Son of God, the Saviour and Helper and Refuge and Rest of all those that are weary in Thy work...... Make perfect with us Thy grace and Thy mercy unto the end, and give us the boldness that is in Thee. Behold, Lord, that Thee alone we love: and behold, Lord, that we have left our homes and the homes of these our kindred, and for Thy sake we are become strangers without compulsion. Behold, Lord, that we have left our possessions for Thy sake, that we might gain Thee, the possession of life, that cannot be taken away. Behold, our Lord, that we have left all our kindred for Thy sake, that we might be united in kinship to Thee. Behold, our Lord, that we have left our fathers and our mothers and our fosterers that we might see Thy exalted Father and be filled with His divine nourishment."

With this we may compare the following sentences from the Apocryphal Gospel:

> " Be Thou to us the head and the overseer and the lord and

the director and the liberator and the Saviour : and in all that is given to us from Thee, in gratitude to Thee let it be *made perfect with us unto the end* of the world.........

"Yea, our God, we beseech, reveal to us in mercies and grace and show us; our Lord, give us our requests for the knowledge and the advantage of those who read and understand : for lo! according to Thy word we have hated the world and all that is therein, *and we have left fathers and race, and have cleaved to Thee who art the Saviour of our race,* the beginning and the end and the guide and the governor of our life. Thy mercies are over the evil and over the good, *and Thou livest and makest to live &c."*

It is perhaps within the bounds of reasonable identification to suggest that the writer of the Gospel and Apocalypses was familiar with the Acts of Thomas, which he has consciously or unconsciously imitated.

THE GOSPEL OF THE TWELVE HOLY APOSTLES TOGETHER WITH THE REVELATIONS OF EACH ONE OF THEM; DONE FROM HEBREW INTO GREEK AND FROM GREEK INTO SYRIAC.

THE beginning of the Gospel of Jesus the Christ, the son of the living God, according as it is said by the Holy Spirit, 'I send an angel before his face, who shall prepare his way.' Mark i. 1.

It came to pass in the 309th year of Alexander the son of Philip the Macedonian, in the reign of Tiberius Caesar, in the government of Herod the ruler of the Jews, that the angel Luke iii. 1. Gabriel, the chief of the angels, by the command of God went down to Nazareth, to a virgin called Mariam of the tribe of Judah Luke i. the son of Israel (her who was betrothed to Joseph the Just), and he appeared to her and said, 'Lo! there ariseth from thee the one that spake with our fathers, and he shall be a Saviour to Israel; and they who do not confess him shall perish, for his authority is in the lofty heights, and his kingdom does not pass away.'

Then Mariam was perturbed at this word, and was exceedingly terrified, and Mariam answered and said, 'And how is it possible that this thing should be as thou hast said, since a man is not known to me, and thou announcest a son to me?'

And the angel said to her, 'Verily, for thus the God of greatness wills it, there comes forthwith the Holy Ghost, and the Lord dwells in thee.'

And Mariam knelt and worshipped God, and said, 'My Lord, may it be unto me according to thy word.'

And Mariam bore a son in Bethlehem of Judah and his name Matt. ii. 1. was called Jesus the Saviour, and the Ruler and the God who is over all: according as the Holy Spirit spake by the mouth of David the prophet; "and he hath put all things under his feet, all Heb. ii. 8.
Ps. viii. sheep and oxen, also the beast of the field, and the fowls that are in heaven and the fish of the sea, which pass through the paths of the seas": and there hath been made subject to him, to this Jesus, all that is in heaven and all that is in the earth.

Matt. ii. And after a short time, viz. eight months, he fled from Herod into Egypt, in order that all things that were written might be fulfilled, and after the death of Herod there appeared an angel unto Joseph, and he brought the boy back to the land of Israel; and he grew and attained to full stature, according as it is written by the four truthful Evangelists; and this is the preaching of the Holy Gospel.

And he wrought in the world great works of power, and plenteous marvels without number; a multitude of which the scribes of the holy Gospel have left [on record]. He healed the sick; he cleansed the lepers; he raised the dead; he opened [the eyes of] the blind; he strengthened the paralytics; he satisfied the hungry; and he wrought miracles. And he chose him true disciples and twelve apostles, that they might be with him, whose names are as follows:

> Simeon, who is called Kepha: he is from the tribe of Reuben:

Mark iii. 17.
> James and John, the sons of Zabdai, they are from the tribe of Issachar:
>
> and Andrew from the tribe of Zebulon:
>
> and Philip from the tribe of Joseph:
>
> and Bar Tholmai from the tribe of Simeon:
>
> and Matthew from the tribe of Naphtali:
>
> and Thomas from the tribe of Benjamin:
>
> and James the son of Alphaeus from the tribe of Levi:
>
> and Thaddaeus from the tribe of Judah:
>
> and Simeon the Canaanite from the tribe of Asher:
>
> and Judas (he that betrayed him) from the tribe of Gad.

Luke xxii. 30. These twelve are his disciples to whom he promised twelve thrones that they may judge Israel.

And it came to pass that when our Lord did all these wonders, and taught the word of God in the synagogues, and in the cities and in the streets, it was evil in the eyes of the elders and the scribes of the people; and they stirred up against him the judges and those that were possessed of authority, until they brought against him accusations, and attestations through their envy, in order that they might destroy him, according as all [his] life is written in the Holy Gospel of the four truthful Evangelists.

And our Lord commanded them and said to them that they should go out and evangelize in the four quarters of the world; and we carried out the preaching[1], lo! from the ends of the earth to the ends of the same. Mark xvi. 15.

But after this, the Jews made a plot against him, the chief-priests and the elders and the scribes of the people, with one of his disciples, him that is called Scariota, and he took money for his price, and delivered him up to them, and they delivered him to the judges and they judged him and crucified him and he died and was buried, and the third day he rose, according as it is written, and [as] he said to his disciples, when he was with them, before he was betrayed. But Judas after the death of the Righteous One, was separated and inherited bitter death by miserable strangling, according to the mystery which our Lord revealed to Simeon Kepha, and to those holy women who were ministering to them before his death. They, when he rose, announced it to the apostles, and the disciples went according to the message which they had received from our Lord, when he was with them, and there they saw him. And there was amongst them one who doubted concerning the resurrection. And the eleven apostles brought in, instead of Judas, Matthias; and he stands in his place, and he was with them, and like unto them, an apostle. Luke viii. 3. Matt. xxviii. 7. Mark xvi. 7.

And he appeared to the eleven when they were reclining at meat, while full of anxieties about stumbling; and he reproached them for their unbelief; and reproved them for their hardness of heart; and he straightway commanded the preachers of the truth, and the proclaimers of the verity, that they should go out into the four quarters [of the world] and preach the Gospel, and baptize and say 'The Kingdom of heaven is come nigh unto you.' And whosoever believeth and heareth shall live for ever. And he said to them, 'In my name they shall cast out devils, they shall speak with new tongues, which they have not known, nor understood, and in my name if they shall drink any deadly poison, it shall not hurt them.' Matt. xxvii. 17. John xx. Acts i. Mark xvi. 14. Mark xvi. 17.

But Jesus, after these words which his disciples heard from him——they say to him, Lo! thou goest away from us and ascendest to him that sent thee, and there is given to thee all power, both in heaven and on earth, and thou hast commanded us that we should preach with new tongues......

[1] See note on p. 14.

And after this [they prayed] the following prayer.

And they said, We beseech thee, our Lord and God not to deprive us of thy grace, but establish us in thy grace and enrich us in knowledge that comes from thee, and cause thy Holy Spirit to dwell in us, and give us the mercies and compassion that come from thyself: and perfect with us the gift that is from thyself; and with those that call truly on thy name, let no error come nigh us, and let not the devil smite us with his destroying arrows: and let us not taste of the poison of the cruel serpent; for this was the cause of the fall of our father Adam. But be thou to us the head and the overseer, and the lord and the director, and the liberator and the Saviour; and in all that is given to us from thee, in gratitude to thee let it be made perfect with us until the end of the world. Yea! our Lord, enrich us according to thy promises, that we may speak with new tongues, by the Spirit that is from thee; and let us know what is the end of the world: because we stand in the midst of offences and scandals of the world; reveal and interpret to us, our Lord, what is the manner of thy coming, and what is the end, and what offences exist in the world; for, lo! thou art taken up from us, and what we shall say we know not.

And Jesus rebuked them and said, Why is all this little-faith of yours? Lo! I have given you my promises, and have fulfilled to you your petitions: and ye shall speak with various tongues, and nothing shall be hidden from you: and I have put the Holy Spirit in you, and my truth have I fixed in your hearts, for profit and for salvation and for the invitation to the Kingdom of Heaven of such as read and hear and do your words. It is not as with other evangelists who talk of what they have seen and repeat what they have heard, but you shall speak, by the Spirit of my Father, of those things that are and of those that are to come. And those who believe and do shall see new life in the kingdom of my Father in Heaven.

And forthwith our Lord was taken up from his twelve [apostles], and their minds were fervent [and were inflamed] like a fire that burns; and there was given to each one of them a tongue and grace, and Simeon spake with them in Hebrew, and James in Latin, and John in Greek, and Andrew in Palestinian, and Philip in Egyptian, and Bar Tholmai in Elamite (?), and Matthew in Parthian, and Thomas in Indian, and James the son of Alpheus in the tongue of Mesopotamia, which is beyond the river, and Thaddaeus in African, and Simeon the Cananaean in Median, and Matthias in the Persian tongue. And they understood what they were saying, each man [understanding] the tongue of his fellow. And all those who heard them, were astonished and perturbed, and they said, ' How have these barbarous and contemptible people suddenly become wise, and speakers of intricate things and revealers of secrets? Who hath given them this, and how have they been instructed? For lo! we hear them speaking with new tongues in which they were not born, and preaching repentance and inviting men to the kingdom of God! Were they not born among us and did they not grow up with us? And they were feeble of understanding, and now we hear from them secret things and revelations such as the tongues of men cannot tell. This cannot be without the finger of God, which has enriched them.' `Acts ii. 8.`

And after that they had taught and admonished the people according as they were commanded by our Lord, [they gathered] `Acts i. 13.` in the upper room where they had been with Jesus and they bowed down and worshipped God : and they all of them besought as with one soul that they might be made perfect each one in the tongue of his fellow and of his discourse ; and that after this with one accord and agreement they might ask from God this gift which was promised to them ; and that there might be a revelation to them concerning the end ; and Simeon Kepha and the eleven disciples bowed down before God in the same upper room and they prayed and besought from God and said the following prayer :

Lord God the Mighty, the Father and Sender of our Lord Jesus Christ, whom thou didst send as thine only Son, to set us free from evil, and from error and to instruct us in the way of life ; we call upon thee, Lord, and we seek of thee that we may be found worthy of the gifts which the holy mouth of our Lord promised to us ; and let us not be deprived of the grace and the mercies which by his promise have lighted upon us; but grant us, Lord, and count us worthy that all of us with one soul and with one mind may see thy revelation, that great and marvellous revelation by which thou art to reveal to us concerning things created, and that we may understand the times before thy coming again, and how they pass away and are no more, and who are the rulers of those [times], and their lives ; and what men are to see the end ; and who is he that is to come as thy adversary and to contend with the truth; and whether all men err from thee and cleave to error; yea, our God, we beseech, reveal to us in mercies and grace and show us: our Lord, give us our requests, for the knowledge and the advantage of those who read and understand; for lo! according to thy word we have hated the world and all that is therein, and we have left fathers and race and have cleaved to thee, who art the Saviour of our race, and the beginning and the end and the guide and the governor of our life: thy mercies are over the good and over the evil; and thou livest and makest to live; and thou hast authority over the exit of all of us; reveal grace to us, show us good, be propitious to thy servants, O Merciful One; and give us in thy holy name to trample on the head of the bitter serpent, thy enemy.

And when they had finished their prayer, forthwith suddenly [the Lord] flashed lightning over them from heaven; and [the earth] was filled with a great light, such as men had never seen before, and like it can never be again, except that light in which our Lord is to be revealed.

And the light tarried over them for three hours, that day being the Friday; and a mighty voice was heard from within the light which said, 'Blessed and blessing is he that came and that comes in the name of the Lord; blessed is the mystery of Salvation.'

Thus they heard until that light faded from the upper room; and suddenly a voice sounded out to them and they heard it saying, 'Go forth to the mountain to the place in which Moses and Elias appeared to you: and there it shall be spoken to you in spirit, concerning the world and the end, and concerning the kingdom of God, and all of you shall speak of it in the tongues of the holy fathers.'

And when the voice was silent, they fell upon their faces from their fear a great and long space; and with the tears from their eyes all the upper room was full of water; and Simeon Kepha and his eleven companions rose up, being bound and called by the Holy Spirit, and they went whither Jesus had directed them, and they were there fasting and praying seven days [? and did eat nothing], and suddenly there were set before them [? tables] full of all good things, things excellent, whence they came our Lord only knows, things from which he himself was nourished; and on the morrow, like as on the first day, he

? Matt. iv. 11.

flashed light over them, and made them fervent in spirit and in truth, and a voice came to them and said, 'Speak out, speak out!' And they began to glorify God and laud and praise and exalt our Lord, asking from him that the gift might be completed [which he had promised].

REVELATION OF SIMEON KEPHA.

And Simeon was moved by the Spirit of God: and his appearance and his body were enlarged, and he glorified [God]; and he wept and said, How great are thy works, O Lord, and all of them thou hast wrought in wisdom. For lo! I see the hosts of God which are a thousand thousands, yea! tens of thousands without number, standing in heaven, and glorifying the lofty throne of the Godhead, exalted above all. And there was sent to me the great angel Michael to be a remembrancer to me, and I received the Spirit in abundance; and I saw the time that is to be after us, full of offences and evils and sins and lying: and the men in that [time] will be crafty, perverse and depraved, men that know not God, and understand not the truth; but a few of them shall understand their God, because of his works which they behold daily, those which are established in heaven, and those which are brought forth on earth; and they know the Lord, as if they did not discern him; for this name only is called upon them that are believers. And after a time they will seek to perform miracles, in the name of our Lord Jesus, and they will not be able, because of their little faith; and they call and are not heard, because they do not call on him with all their hearts. But those who are separated from them, few in number, ask and are heard because their hearts speak the truth, and know God, and understand his beloved Son, and do not deny the Spirit. And in this way they perform signs and great works of power; and these also in their wealth and in their faith are not suffered to live; for there will rise up against them bribed judges and also bribed deniers [of the faith]; and for the name of our Lord they shall be judged and beaten; and they will kill them by bitter and various deaths: and also after that they are killed they shall perform by their death great works of power; and after these things shall have happened, the faith shall fail from the earth and orthodoxy shall come to an end : and those who are named as being baptised in our Lord and as confessing his name, shall be more miserable than all men ; and they shall trample on the faith and talk perversely and they shall divide our Lord ; and in that time there shall be reckoned many teachers, as the Spirit of the Father does not speak in them, and they shall divide our Lord ; and the father of lies and the calumniator, that is, Satan, shall enter into them and disturb their minds ; and their faith shall fail and it will come to pass that when they rise up and tear it, and when every man in his place will say that I am superior in the fear of God, and I confess him more correctly, that they shall seek our Lord and shall not find him, and they will call to him and he will not answer them. And the Lord will deliver them to evils and to misery and to wrath and to pillage and to tribute, until they shall ask death for themselves and shall not find a saviour, and they shall be enraged and blaspheme against God, and they shall say, ' Because we have the superior knowledge of God on this account the more have evils tracked our steps'; [but] the few who shall be scattered in the countries, who confess the Son in the way that is right for them to do, of these the Lord shall supply their needs ; but those who do not believe in him, and who are called baptised people shall felicitate the heathen, and they shall envy them and shall say, ' Why are these things so, and why has it been given to us on this wise ? ' And even those who preach among them, on whom the name of the Lord was called, in the headship over their brethren and in the offices of the Church will be disturbers and self-exalting persons and haters one of another : lovers of money and destroyers of order, and who do not keep the commandments : but they will not love their flocks, and in their days men will appear as sheep who are ravening wolves, and they will eat up the labour of the orphans, and the sustenance of the widows, and every ruler shall pervert justice, and their eyes shall be blinded by bribery, and they shall love vainglory, and because of all these evils that are performed by them, they shall call upon the Lord, and there will be none to answer them, and there will be no Saviour for them ; because evils are multiplied on the earth, and they have corrupted their ways before the Father in Heaven ; and the destroyer shall deliver them up to devastation, and to misery, and to necessity, and there shall rise up against them wasps in the morning and in the evening, and shall oppress them ;

and men shall see their sons and their daughters and their wives and their revenues made a prey by their enemies; and there will be none that speaks and none that answers, because the Holy One wills it, and the Lofty One talks with them; and from before him judgment shall go forth, and they shall bring upon them all these evils, and they will light upon them, until they shall return and become one true flock and one holy church, and they shall confess our Lord according as we received from him, and according as we believed in the Son the Life-Giver and Saviour of the world; and after this will be a flock and a church and a baptism, true and one: and it will come to pass in that day, that every one that shall call on the name of the Lord shall be saved, and whosoever worships the Paraclete shall be delivered.

Revelation of James the Apostle.

And the angel departed from Simeon and drew near to James; and he was shaken by the Spirit of God, and he wept and wailed and said, 'Alas! our Lord Jesus, for the desolation that I see in this holy city: for lo! after a certain time the temple will be laid waste, the house of the Lord, the great and renowned; and the city Jerusalem shall be laid waste; and it shall be perturbed and shall become a place of pollution; and it shall be delivered up to a people that knoweth not God and doth not understand the truth; because of the wickedness of them that dwell therein; in that they have blasphemed the name of our Lord Jesus, and have crucified and killed him.' And again the apostle James was astonied and said, 'Lo, I see that there comes against her a man renowned in name and fearsome in appearance, and he will devastate, and extirpate and destroy them that dwell therein; and there shall be in it much dearth and wrath; and the God of heaven shall be wroth with them; and the eyes of their hearts shall be darkened and they shall not see the sun; and they shall not understand the marvels of the Lord; because they have not known his Son; and because of their want of intelligence they shall perish; and he shall banish them that dwell in her, and shall kill and shall destroy, and there shall not be found in her any except them that wail and that weep; and after all these things have happened to the city of the Lord, there shall come forth a man who oppresses them by war against his enemies, and in that war he shall die; and there shall be in authority over her another man, and he shall set up his edicts, and shall settle her, and there shall be built in her sanctuaries to the Lord, consecrated and renowned, and they shall come from the ends of the earth and from its bounds; and of all them that hear the name of the Lord and know his praises, men shall worship there the Lord the Holy One, and they shall offer there vows and odours and sacrifices and libations, and the Lord shall set up therein a sign that overcomes the evil of the wicked, and no man shall grudge thereat nor be evil affected: for there will be therein another house of worship, because peace is decreed to her by the Holy One of Israel; and a great and renowned house shall be built in her at great cost, with gold of Ophir, and beryls of Havilah, and its name shall go forth and be renowned, more than all those houses in the earth: and they shall say that never before it [was there such], and never after will it be so. And that king who began to build it, shall die on the completion of his building: and one from his seed shall rise up in his place, and shall burden the chief men with many ills; and he shall have great and vigorous rule, and the earth shall be governed in his days in great peace: because from God it has been so spoken concerning him and concerning his people by the mouth of the prophet Daniel: and it shall come to pass that whosoever shall call upon the name of the Lord he will save.'

REVELATION OF JOHN THE LITTLE THE BROTHER OF JAMES, AND THEY TWO ARE THE SONS OF ZABDAI.

And there was suddenly a great earthquake, and John the brother of James, and the initiate[1] of our Lord, fell on his face on the earth, and with a great trembling he worshipped God the Lord of all; and our Lord sent to him a man in white raiment, and mounted on a horse of fire, and his appearance was like the flashing of fire; and he touched him, and set him up and said to him, 'John, behold thou hast been set by our Lord to preach the Gospel of Salvation, along with the three that perform the truth; but ye also shall not be deprived of this gift;

[1] Lit. *son of the mysteries.*

for there hath been given unto thee the Spirit, that thou shouldst receive it in double measure: because more than thy first companions thou hast known the mysteries of our Saviour': and John was moved by the Holy Spirit and was made fervent and said, 'Lo! I see heaven opened and holy ones who are in the lofty heights in appearance like lightning, and glorifying God the maker of all.' And I beheld and an angel approached me, one of those that are near to him; and he brought me scrolls written with the finger of truth, and inscribed in them times and generations, and the iniquities and sins of men; and the miseries that are to come on the earth; and I arose as it were stupefied. And there was a voice exceeding dread, which said, 'Let the mysteries be revealed that are hidden from the beginning, in soul and in spirit.' And the angel of God who was sent to me touched me and said to me, 'Open thy mouth and receive'; and I opened my mouth and I beheld and he put therein some- Exod. xvi. thing like beryls and white like snow: and its taste was very $\frac{31.}{Num. xi.}$ sweet and I ate it. And he said to me, 'Behold, it is the day of 7. salvation, and the hour of deliverance! Speak, for the Lord hath pleasure in thee! Speak, O man, to whom has been given power over the mysteries of God! Speak without fear, for it is the will of God, that the secret things should be expounded to thee.' And I beheld that there was written on the scrolls what men are to suffer in the last times: and when I saw all these things that are past, I was not willing to speak concerning them, but only that I should expound those things that are to come; and there was a voice which spake in me, Woe, woe to the sons of men who are left to the generations [and] to the times that are to come! For there shall rise up the kings of the north and they shall become strong and shall shake the whole world, and there shall be amongst them a man who subdues all the peoples by the marvellous sign which appeared to him in heaven, and he shall be prosperous and it shall go well with him; and after him shall rise up kings of the Romans; insolent, evil, idol-worshipping, godless; accusers and plotters and accepters of persons; and all the people of the Romans shall fall into fornication and adultery, and they shall love bribery and lasciviousness through the abundance of wine that they drink; and while their power is over all the world, because of their evil sins and blasphemies against God, the Lord shall send wrath upon them from heaven, and Persia

shall become strong against them and shall drive away and expel
this kingdom from the world, because it hath done evil exceedingly, and kings shall rise up among them great and renowned,
and lovers of money, and they shall take away government from
the earth : and there shall be one of them who because of his
love of money shall destroy many men, until commerce and trade
shall perish from off the whole earth, and by the son of his own
body[1] he shall die; and all the silver and gold that he has
collected shall not save him; and after this Persia shall rule for
a little time, and it also shall be delivered over to Media[2]; because
of their evil sins the God of heaven shall abolish their rule, and
shall destroy their kingdom; and they shall perish and cease
to be.

But there will be deniers of the truth, and men that know
not God, and that do corruptly in their lasciviousness, those who
provoke God, and then suddenly shall be fulfilled the prophecy of
Daniel the pure and the desired, which he spake, that God shall
send forth a mighty wind, the Southern one; and there shall
come forth from it a people of deformed aspect, and their appearance and manners like those of women; and there shall rise up
from among them a warrior, and one whom they call a prophet,
and they shall be brought into his hands...... those like to
whom there has not been any in the world neither do there exist
their like; and every one that hears shall shake his head and
shall deride him and say, 'Why doth he speak thus? And
God seeth it and regardeth it not.'

And the South shall do prosperously, and by the hoofs
of the horses of his armies they shall trample down Persia
and subdue it and devastate Rome; and there shall not be
found any that stands before them, because it has been ordained
for them by the Holy One of Heaven; and it shall come to
pass that every kingdom or people or place that hears the
report of them shall be afraid and shall tremble and shall be
terrified at the report of this people, until it shall subdue and
bring under its hands the whole earth; and twelve renowned
kings shall rise up from that people according as it is written
in the law when God talked with Abraham and said to him, 'Lo!
Concerning Ishmael thy son I have heard thee, and twelve

---

[1] Lit. *side*.   [2] Query *tribute*.

princes shall he beget along with many other princesses'; and he, even he, is the people of the land of the South. He shall lead captive a great captivity amongst all the peoples of the earth and they shall spoil a great spoil, and all the ends of the earth shall do service and there shall be made subject to him many lordships; and his hand shall be over all, and also those that are under his hand he shall oppress with much tribute: and he shall oppress and kill and destroy the [rulers of the] ends [of the earth]. And he shall impose a tribute on [the earth], such as was never heard of; until a man shall come out from his house, and shall find [there] four collectors who collect tribute; and men shall sell their sons and daughters because of their need: and they shall hate their lives and shall wail and weep, and there is no voice nor discourse except Woe, Woe! and they shall be covetous with a hateful cupidity: and they will be converted like bridegrooms and like brides, but......will dread some requital from them; because he that has shall be reckoned in their days as though he had not, and he that builds and he that sells as one that gets no gain; and there shall prosper with them all those who take refuge with them, and they shall enslave to them men renowned in race, and there shall be among them hypocrites and men who know not God, and regard not men, except prodigals, fornicators Luke xviii. and men wicked and revengeful.

But woe! woe! to the children of men in that time; and they shall rule in a cave[1] for one great week and the half of a great week; and every king who shall arise from amongst them shall strengthen and be made strong, and shall be more vigorous than his fellow; and they shall gather together the gold of the earth: and they shall descend and lay them up in the earth treasures which came forth therefrom; because their kingdom and authority is from God...and it shall come to pass after the week and the half of a week the earth shall be moved concerning them, and God shall require the sins of creation at their hands; and the South wind shall subside, and God shall bring to nought their covenant with them; and they shall tremble and be affrighted at every report that is brought to them; and the hands of all flesh shall be upon them; according as it was said by the hand of Moses the servant of the Lord; and in the end of their times

---

[1] Read *over the world*.

f

they shall do evil to all flesh that is under their power, and they shall oppress and enslave and ravage, and men shall see necessity and great affliction: and three and four of them shall be associated in pollution. And there is none that speaks and none that hears, except only one that says, Woe! woe! what is come to pass in our generation! And they shall felicitate the dead of ancient time, and shall ask for death for themselves, and there is none that redeems and none that replies: but so much the more will they afflict all of those who confess our Lord Christ; because they shall hate to the very end the name of the Lord, and shall bring to nought his covenant; and truth shall not be found amongst them, but only villainy shall they love and sin shall they have an affection for. And whatever is hateful in the eyes of the Lord that will they do: and they shall be called a corrupt people; and after these things the Lord shall be angered against them, as he was against Rome, and against Media and Persia; and straightway there will come upon them the end, and suddenly the time [comes]; and at last in the completion of the week and a half God shall stir up against them desolation; and an angel of wrath shall descend, and shall kindle evil amongst them; and......in their midst; and they shall be lifted up one against the other, and they shall make and become two parties, and each party shall seek to call himself king, and there shall be war between them, and there shall be many murders by them and among them, and much blood shall be shed among them at the fountain of waters which is in the place which was spoken of beforetime in the book of the Sibyl (?). And when the man of the North shall hear this report, he shall not be affrighted, and he shall say, By my might and by my arm have I overcome. Then shall he associate with him all the peoples of the earth, and he will go forth against him, and they shall destroy and devastate his armies and lead captive their sons and their daughters and their wives, and there shall fall upon them a bitter wedlock and misery; and the Lord shall cause the spirit of the South to return to his place from whence he came forth, and shall bring to nought his name and his fame; and it shall come to pass that when they shall enter again the place from whence they came out, the enemy shall not pursue them thither, and they shall not fear hunger and they shall not tremble, and it shall come to pass in that day that their reliance [shall be] upon silver which they have gotten by wrong and by plunder which they have hidden in the place named Diglath, and they shall return and settle in the land from whence they came out; and God shall stir up for them there evil times and times of plagues, and without war they shall be laid waste, and unto all generations of the world there shall not be among them any that holds a weapon and stands up in battle......

......which the Father commanded concerning them from Heaven [and when] John had spoken these words and visions and revelations in truth, the angel that spake (?) to him departed from him, and a voice said, Suffer thy companions[1]......that they may talk with thee.

[1] Or perhaps : Leave [thy scrolls] to thy companions.

Then follows an extract from the Doctrine of Addai.

f. 58 a [.
[1] Cod.   [2] Cod.   [3] Second hand, as it seems: first hand illegible.

Then follows an extract from the Teaching of Addai.

ܠܗܘܢ܂ ܘܢܗܘܘܢ ܐܪ̈ܕܝܐ ܕܟܠ ܒܗܪ ܒܗܘܢ܂ ܐܝܟ
ܕܐܡܪܝܢ ܒܐܢܫ̈ܐ ܕܡܘܫܚܐ ܒܒ̈ܢܘܗ ܕܡܪ̈ܕܝܐ. ܘܒܗ
ܒܟܠܗܘܢ ܕܒܗܘܢ܂ ܢܒܐܫܘܢ ܠܟܠܒܗܪ ܕܐܝܬ ܒܫܘܠܛܢܗܘܢ܂
ܘܢܐܠܨܘܢ ܘܢܫܥܒܕܘܢ ܘܢܒܗܘܢ ܘܢܚܪܘܢ ܒܒ̈ܢܝܢܫܐ
ܐܢܫܐ ܘܐܘܠܨܢܐ ܪܒܐ. ܘܢܬܬܘܬܒܘܢ ܬܠܬܐ ܘܐܪ̈ܒܥܐ
ܡܢܗܘܢ ܐܒܫܪܐ ܒܠܒܘܬܐ. ܘܠܝܬ ܕܐܡܪ ܘܠܐ
ܕܫܡܥ. ܐܠܐ ܕܐܡܪ ܗܘ ܘ. ܡܢܐ ܗܘܐ ܒܕܪ܂
ܘܢܬܠܘܢ ܠܒܒܐ ܠܡܬ̈ܪܬܐ ܕܡܢ ܟܠܗ ܘܢܫܐܠܘܢ ܡܟܬܐ
ܠܢܫܬܗܘܢ܂ ܘܠܝܬ ܕܦܪܩ ܘܠܐ ܕܒܥܐ. ܢܐܠܨܘܢ
ܬܬܪܐܝܬ ܠܟܠܗܘܢ ܐܝܟ ܕܡܘܕܝܢ ܒܡܫܝܚܐ ܡܪ܂
ܡܛܠ ܕܢܫܘܢ ܠܫܪܬܐ ܫܡܗ ܕܡܪܝܐ. ܘܢܒܛܠܘܢ
ܡܢܗ. ܘܫܪܪܐ ܠܐ ܢܬܒܥ ܒܗܘܢ ܐܠܐ ܒܢ̈ܬܬܐ
ܢܦܫܗܘܢ܂ ܘܣܦܝܩܬܐ ܢܣܒܘܢ܂ ܘܟܠ ܕܗܘܢܐ ܒܒ̈ܢܝ ܡܕܝܢܐ
ܫܦܪܘܢ܂ ܘܒܟܠܐ ܦܠܓܐ ܢܬܟܠܘܢ. ܘܡܢ ܒܬܪ ܗܠܝܢ
ܢܦܠ ܡܕܝܢܐ ܒܠܒܗܘܢ܂ ܐܝܟ ܕܟܠ ܪܘܫܥܐ. ܘܡܕܝ
ܘܦܪܣ. ܘܡܫܝܚܐ ܗܕܝܢ ܢܦܠܓܐ ܒܠܒܗܘܢ ܡܢ ܘܒܪܝܐ
ܡܢ ܥܠܝܐ ܘܠܫܪܬܐ ܒܫܘܠܛ ܥܡܘܡܐ ܘܡܠܟܗ. ܢܓܪܐ
ܒܗܘܢ ܐܠܗܐ ܫܪܒܐ ܘܢܫܘܬ ܡܠܐܟܐ ‖ ܕܪܘܓܙܐ f. 57 b
ܘܢܦܕܫ ܒܗܘܢ ܒܢܫܬܐ.... ܒܢܬܗܘܢ ܒܓܘܗܘܢ܂
ܘܢܬܬܪܢܡܘܢ ܫ̣ ܒ[ܡ] ܫ̣ ܘܢܒܒܕܘܢ ܘܢܗܘܘܢ ܬ̈ܪܝܢ
ܓܒ̈ܐ. ܘܢܒܒܐ ܟܠܫ ܡܢܗܘܢ ܕܗܘ ܢܫܡܗ ܢܦܫܐ
ܡܠܟܐ. ܘܦܪܟܐ ܢܗܘܐ ܒܢܬܗܘܢ܂ ܘܩ̈ܛܠܐ ܦܓܪ̈ܐ
ܡܢܗܘܢ ܘܒܗܘܢ܂ ܘܕܡܐ ܪܒܐ ܢܬܐܕ ܒܗܘܢ ܟܠ
ܚܢܐ ܕܡ̈ܪܝܐ ܕܐܝܬ ܒܕܘܒܬܐ ܗܝ ܕܡܫܕܡܐ ܐܡܪܝܐ

---

[1] The text is corrupt.

ܡܢܗ̇ ܒܥܠܡܐ ܡܫܒܪ ܒܚܝܘܬܐ. ܕܚܝܘܗ ܘܕܘܒܪ̈ܘܗܝ، ܐܝܟ
ܕ̈ܝܢܐ. ܘܢܦܘܩ ܒܗܘܢ ܠܒܪܐ ܡܪܒܬܢܐ ܘܕܡܫܬܒܚܝܢ
ܠܗ ܠܒܢܝܐ. ܘܢܬܬܘܢ ܒܟ̈ܘܕܘܗܝ، ‖ . . . . ܐܝܠܝܢ ܕܠܐ f. 56 a
ܗܘܐ ܒܥܠܡܐ ܐܒܗܬܗܘܢ ܘܠܐ ܕܕܚܝܢ ܗܘܘ ܠܗܘܢ. ܕܟܠ
ܡܢ ܕܫܡܥ ܚܝܠ ܪܒܗ. ܘܢܚܡ ܘܢܐܡܪ. ܕܠܡܢܐ ܗܟܢܐ
ܡܡܠܠ ܗܢܐ. ܘܚܙܐ ܐܠܗܐ ܘܡܫܡܫܢܐ. ܘܐܬܓܠܝ ܗܘ،
ܬܫܒܘܚܬܐ. ܘܒܦܪܘܫܬܐ ܕܢ̈ܒܝܐ ܕܫܠܝܚܘܬܗܘܢ ܘܕܪܘܫܘܢ
ܠܦܪܘ ܘܢܫܒܚܘܢܗ̇ ܘܢܫܪܒܘܢ ܠܪܗܘܡܝܐ. ܘܠܐ ܢܬܚܡܣ
ܕܡܐܩ ܡܕܡܫܝܚܘܢ؛ ܡܛܠ ܕܡܢ ܡܕܝܢܐ ܕܫܡܝܐ ܐܬܦܩܕ.
ܠܗܘܢ؛ ܘܢܗܘܐ ܕܟܠ ܡܠܟܘܬܐ ܐܘ ܥܡܐ ܐܘ ܐܬܪܐ
ܕܢܬܒܥ ܫܡܫܗܘܢ ܢܫܩܠ ܘܢܗܘܒ ܘܢܣܬܪ. ܡܢ ܫܡܫܗ
ܕܒܥܡܐ ܗܘ. ܒܪܥܡܐ ܠܚܠܘܗ̇ ܐܪܒܐ ܢܫܒܘܩ ܘܢܒܒܪܘܢ
ܬܫܢܬ ܐܬ̈ܪܘܗܝ. ܘܕܬܬܒܥܪ ܡܠܟ̈ܐ ܡܫ̈ܡܫܐ ܢܗܘܡܘܢ
ܡܢܗ ܐܝܟ ܡܐ ܕܟܬܝܒ ܒܐܘܪܝܬܐ. ܟܕ ܡܠܠ ܐܠܗܐ
ܥܡ ܐܒܪܗܡ ܘܐܡܪ ܠܗ. ܕܗܐ ܥܠ ܐܫܡܥܝܠ ܒܪܟ
ܫܡܥܬܟ. ܘܬܪܥܣܪ ܪ̈ܘܪܒܢܐ ܢܘܠܕ. ܥܡ ܐܚܪ̈ܢܝܬܐ
ܦܓܪ̈ܐܬܐ. ܘܗܘ ܟܕ ܗܘ ܒܥܡܐ ܕܐܪܒܐ ܕܬܫܡܫܬܐ.
ܢܒܥܐ ܥܒܝܬܐ ܪܒܬܐ ܒܥܠܡܐ ܒܡ̈ܥܡܐ ܕܐܪܒܐ
ܘܢܒܘܘܢ ܒܝܬܐ ܘܒܠܗܝܢ ܦܢ̈ܝܬܐ ܕܐܪܒܐ ܬ̈ܥܠܝܡ
ܒܒܕܘܬܐ ܘܢܫܬܥܒܕܘܢ ܠܗ ܡܕܝ̈ܢܬܐ ܦܠ̈ܓܘܬܐ. ܘܬܗܘܐ
ܐܚܪܗ ܥܠ ܟܠ ܘܐܦ ܠܐܝܠܝܢ ܕܐܝܬ ܬܫܝܬ ܐܚܪܗ
ܢܐܠܦܝܢ ܡܕܐܬܐ ܦܠܓܐܬܐ ‖ ܘܢܐܠܦܝܢ ܘܢܦܩܠ ܘܢܩܒ. f. 56 b
ܬ̈ܠ[ܝܐ. . . .] ܕܦܢ̈ܝܬܐ. ܘܢܥܕܐ ܡܕܐܬܐ ܥܠ . . . . ܐܚܕܐ
ܕܠܐ ܐܫܬܡܥܬ ܐܒܗܬܗ̇. ܒܕܡܐ ܕܢܦܩܘ ܠܒܪܐ ܡܢ ܠܗ

f. 55 b

 ||
[1] sic

ܫܡܝܐ ܕܦܬܝܚܝܢ. ܘܡܕ̈ܢܚܐ ܕܒܡܪ̈ܘܡܐ ܚ̈ܝܠܐ ܕܡܫ̈ܒܚܝܢ
ܒܫܘܒܚܗܘܢ ܘܡܫܒܚܝܢ ܠܐܠܗܐ ܒܪܘܝܐ ܕܟܠ. ܘܚܙܝܬ
ܕܡܪܝ. ܡܠܐܟܐ ܡܢ ܗܠܝܢ ܕܡܪܝܒܝܢ ܠܗ. ܘܐܢܬ، ܒܪ̈ܟܐ[1]
ܕܩ̈ܝܡܝܢ ܒܡܨܥܬܐ ܕܩܘܕܫܬܐ. ܘܪ̈ܫܝܡܝܢ ܒܗܘܢ ܐ̈ܦܝܐ
ܘܕܪ̈ܐ. ܘܒܥ̈ܠܝܐ ܘܫܘܦܪܐ ܕܒܢ̈ܝܢܫܐ. ܘܒܢܝܫܬܐ ܕܒܬܪܟܘܢ
ܥܠ ܐܪܥܐ. ܘܡܫܟܬ ܒܪ ܬܘܪ ܐܢܐ. ܘܩܠܐ ܗܘܐ
ܕܕܚܝܠ ܗܘܐ ܠܝ. ܕܐܡܪ ܢܬܟܠܘܢ ܐ̈ܪܙܐ ܕܒܫܡܝܢ ܡܢ
ܩܕܡܝ. ܒܢܦܫ ܘܒܓܘܫ. ܘܩܪܒ ܠܘܬܝ ܡܠܐܟܐ ܕܐܠܗܐ
ܕܐܫܬܕܪ ܠܐܪ̈ܙܝ، ܘܐܡܪ ܠܝ. ܦܬܚ ܦܘܡܟ ܘܡܠܠ.
ܘܦܬܚܬ ܦܘܡܝ. || ܘܚܙܝܬ ܕܗܐ ܒܗ ܡܕܡ ܕܕܡܐ f. 55 a
ܠܒܪ̈ܘܩܐ. ܘܫܦܝܪ ܐܝܟ ܬܠܓܐ. ܘܠܒܫܗ ܠܒ. ܘܠܐ ܗܘܐ
ܘܐܢܐ ܐܠܬܗ. ܘܐܡܪ ܠܝ. ܗܐ ܢܘܗܪܐ ܕܦܘܪܩܢܐ.
ܘܡܫܬܐ ܕܫܘܒܚܐ. ܡܠܠ ܡܛܠ ܕܢܓܕܐ ܒܝ ܡܪܝܐ.
ܡܠܠ ܠܒܪܐ ܕܐܫܬܠܛ ܥܠ ܐ̈ܪܙܘܗܝ ܕܐܠܗܐ. ܡܠܠ
ܕܠܐ ܕܢܠܐ ܡܛܠ ܕܢܓܕܐ ܕܐܠܗܐ ܗܘܐ. ܕܒܫܪ̈ܬܐ
ܢܬܦܫܩܘܢ ܠܝ. ܘܚܙܝܬ ܕܒܬܪ ܒܪ̈ܟܐ[2] ܗܠܝܢ ܡܕܡ
ܕܒܬܪܝܢ ܒܢ̈ܝܢܫܐ ܕܢܫܒܩܘܢ ܒܚܙܬ ܐ̈ܪܥܐ. ܘܒܪ ܚܙܝܬ
ܠܗܠܝܢ ܟܠܗܘܢ ܕܒܚܝܪ̈ܢ ܠܐ ܢܓܚܬ ܕܐܡܠܠ ܟܠܗܘܢ.
ܐܠܐ ܕܐܦܫܘ ܠܐܝܠܝܢ ܕܒܬܪ ܠܡܐܬܐ. ܘܗܘܐ
ܩܠܐ ܕܐܡܪ ܒܝ. ܘܝ، ܘܝ، ܠܒܢ̈ܝܢܫܐ ܕܡܫܬܚܪܝܢ ܠܕ̈ܪܐ
ܠܕ̈ܘܪܐ ܕܒܬܪܝܢ ܠܡܐܬܐ. ܢܩܘܡܘܢ ܓܒܪ ܡܠ̈ܟܐ
ܕܓܢ̈ܒܐ. ܘܢܬܩܦܘܢ ܘܢܚܒܘܢ ܠܡܬܕܒܪܢܘܬܐ ܟܠܗ.
ܘܢܗܘܐ ܒܗܘܢ ܓܒܪܐ ܕܡܫܥܒܕ ܠܟܠܗܘܢ ܒܡܥ̈ܒܕܐ
ܒܐܬܐ ܕܬܕܡܘܪܬܐ ܕܡܬܚܙܝܐ ܠܗ ܒܫܡܝܐ ܘܢܓܠܝ.

[1] Cod. ܒܒܪ̈ܐ [2] Cod. ܒܒܒܪ̈ܐ

ܕܫܘܠܛܐ. ܘܢܐܙܠ ܥܡܗ ܘܢܫܬܡܫܗ. ܝܬܝܪ ܡܢ ܟܠܗܘܢ
ܒܬ̈ܐ ܕܐܪܥܐ. ܘܢܐܡܪܘܢ ܕܠܐ ܡܕܡܗܘ، ܘܠܐ ܒܬܪܗ
ܢܗܘܐ ܗܕܝܐ. ܘܡܠܟܐ ܐܝܢܐ ܕܥܒܪ، ܒܗ ܕܒܝܫܘܗ،
ܒܥܘܠܡ ܟܝܢܗ ܢܗܘܬ. ܘܢܦܘܩ ܡܢ ܙܒܢܗ ܫܠܛܢܗ،.
ܘܒܫܢܬܐ ܫܒܥܝܢܝܬܐ ܠܐܢ̈ܫܐ ܪ̈ܘܪܒܐ ܢܦܠ. ܘܢܗܘܐ ܠܗ
ܫܘܠܛܢܐ ܪܒܐ ܘܬܫܒܘܚܬܐ ܘܬܬܡܠܟܢ[1] ܐܪܥܐ ܒܫܘ̈ܬܬܗ
ܒܫܝܢܐ ܪܒܐ. ܡܛܠ ܕܡܢ ܐܠܗܐ ܐܬܡܠܠ ܥܠܘܗܝ.
ܘܥܠ ܥܡܗ ܒܦܘܡܗ ܕܕܢܝܐܝܠ ܢܒܝܐ. ܘܢܗܘܐ ܥܠ
ܕܡܘܕܐ ܒܥܡܗ ܕܡܕܝܢܐ ܢܐܫܐ

ܓܠܝܢܐ ܕܝܘܚܢܢ ܙܥܘܪܐ ܐܚܘܗܝ ܕܝܥܩܘܒ
ܕܐܝܬܝܗܘܢ ܒܢ̈ܝ ܙܒܕܝ

f. 54 b ܘܗܘܐ ܘܒܬܪ ܙܒܢܐ ‖ ܡܢ ܫܠܝܐ ܘܢܦܠ ܝܘܚܢܢ ܐܚܘܗܝ،
ܘܒܪ ܐܪܐܗ ܕܡܪܢ ܥܠ ܐܦ̈ܘܗܝ، ܥܠ ܐܪܥܐ ܘܒܟܝܬܐ
ܪܒܬܐ ܦܓܥ ܠܐܠܗܐ ܡܪܐ ܟܠ. ܘܐܡܪ ܡܪܝ ܠܘܬܗ
ܡܪܝܐ ܠܥܒܕܐ ܫܘܪܐ ܕܚܒܝܒ ܪܚܡܐ ܕܚܘܪܐ. ܘܚܘܪܗ
ܐܝܟ ܒܪܘܩܐ ܕܚܘܪܐ. ܘܩܪܒ[2] ܠܘܬܗ ܘܐܩܝܡܗ ܘܐܡܪ
ܠܗ. ܝܘܚܢܢ ܗܐ ܐܬܬܦܩܕܬ ܡܢ ܡܪܝ ܕܐܒܪܙ ܦܪܝܫܬܐ
ܕܦܘܪܫܢܐ ܡܢ ܬܠܬܐ ܦܠܓ̈ܝ ܡܘܫܬܐ. ܐܠܐ ܘܐܦ
ܡܢ ܗܕܐ ܡܗܝܡܢܘܬܐ ܠܐ ܬܬܟܠܘܢ܆ ܐܬܝܗܒ ܠܝ
ܥܠ ܪܘܚܐ ܕܒܟܐܦܐ ܬܩܒܠ. ܡܛܠ ܕܒܬܪ ܡܢ ܫܒ̈ܝܠܢ
ܡܕܡ̈ܝܢܐ ܐܝܟܢ ܙܘܪܐ ܕܦܪܘܩ. ܘܐܬܬܝܗܒ ܒܪܘܚܐ
ܡܕܝܢܐ ܝܘܚܢܢ ܘܐܬܦܢܝ ܘܐܡܪ. ܗܐ ܚܙܐ ܐܢܐ

[1] Cod. ܘܬܬܡܠܟܢ [2] MS. ܩܪܒܗ

f. 54 a

ܓܠܝܢܐ ܕܝܥܩܘܒ ܫܠܝܚܐ ܟ

ܐܢܘܢ ܡܫܒܠܢܐ ܠܡܪܝܐ ܘܠܙܘܘܓܐ. ܘܠܐܢܫܐ
ܘܠܡܙܡܪܘܢ ܕܟܢܪ̈ܐ ܩܝܬܪܐ ܘܒܙܡܪܐ ܒܠܝܗܘܢ
ܘܢܐܠܦܘܢ ܐܢܘܢ: ܘܢܣܒܘܢ ܒܒܢ̈ܝܢܫܐ ܒ̈ܢܝܗܘܢ
ܘܒ̈ܢܬܗܘܢ ܘܢܫ̈ܝܗܘܢ ܘܒܬܘܠܬܗܘܢ ܒܙ ܡܬܒܥܝܢ ܡܢ
ܒܠܒܒܗܘܢ: ܘܠܝܬ ܕܐܡܪ ܘܠܝܬ ܕܒܥܐ. ܡܛܠ
ܕܢܫܐ ܝܗܒܐ. ܘܡܙܕܪܟܐ ܡܠܠ ܒܫܡܗ: ܘܡܢ ܕܡܕܡܗܝ،
ܢܦܩ ܕܝܢܐ. ܘܢܬܘܢ ܒܠܝܗܘܢ ܒܠܗܝܢ ܥ̈ܢܝܬܐ. ܘܢܙܥܡ
ܐܢܘܢ: ܒܕܡܐ ܕܢܦܫܗܘܢ ܘܢܣܒܘܢ ܣܓܐ ܡܪܟܒܬܐ
ܙܢܝܘܬܐ. ܘܣܓܐ ܒܙܢܬܐ ܡܕܝܢܬܐ ܘܢܘܕܘܢ ܒܡܪ
ܐܝܟ ܡܐ ܕܣܝܡ ܘܒܠܡ ܡܢܗ. ܘܡܗܝܡܢ ܒܒܪܗ ܡܫܝܚܐ
ܘܦܪܘܩܐ ܕܥܠ̈ܡܐ. ܘܟܬܪܝܢ ܬܗܘܐ ܡܪܟܒܬܐ ܘܥܕܬܐ
ܘܡܫܡܫܢܘܬܐ ܙܢܝܘܬܐ ܣܓܐ. ܘܢܗܘܐ ܒܢܫܐ ܗܘ.
ܘܟܠ ܕܢܦܪܐ ܒܫܡܗ ܕܡܪܝܐ ܢܚܐ. ܘܕܓܠ ܠܗ
ܠܦܪܘܠܝܛܐ ܢܬܘܒ..

ܓܠܝܢܐ ܕܝܥܩܘܒ ܫܠܝܚܐ ||

f. 53 b ܘܦܪܩ ܡܠܐܟܐ ܡܢ ܠܘܬ ܫܡܥܘܢ ܘܗܦܟ ܠܘܬ
ܝܥܩܘܒ. ܘܐܬܬܥܝܪ ܒܪܘܚܐ ܕܐܠܗܐ ܘܒܟܐ ܘܐܡܠܠ.
ܘܐܡܪ. ܐܘܗ ܡܪܢ ܝܫܘܥ ܠܡܪܝܐ ܗܢܐ ܕܚܙܐ ܐܢܐ
ܒܡܕܝܢܬܐ ܗܕܐ ܡܕܝܢܬܐ. ܗܐ ܓܒܪ ܡܢ ܒܬܪ ܘܒܢܝܐ
ܢܒܢܐ ܗܝܟܠ ܢܣܒ ܒܝܬܗ ܕܡܪܝܐ ܪܒܐ ܘܡܫܒܚܐ.
ܘܡܕܝܢܬܐ ܐܘܪܫܠܡ ܬܬܒܢܐ. ܘܬܫܬܟܠܠ. ܘܬܬܗܘܐ ܒܝܬܐ
ܕܡܫܝܚܘܬܐ. ܘܬܫܬܠܛ ܠܥܡܐ ܕܠܐ ܝܕܥ ܠܐܠܗܐ. ܘܠܐ

ܕܢܒܥܘܢܝܗ، ܠܡܪܢ ܘܠܐ ܢܫܡܥܘܢܝܗ، ܘܢܛܪܘܢܝܗ، ܘܠܐ
ܢܕܢܐ ܐܢܘܢ܆ ܘܢܫܠܡ ܐܢܘܢ ܡܪܝܐ ܠܒܝܫܬܐ. ܘܠܙܘܥܐ
ܘܠܪܘܓܙܐ ܘܠܒܘܫܬܐ ܘܠܡܕܐܬܐ. ܒܕܡܐ ܕܢܐܬܠܘܢ
ܡܘܬܐ ܠܢܦ̈ܫܬܗܘܢ ܘܠܐ ܢܚܙܘܢ ܦܪܘܩܐ.
ܘܢܬܪܥܡܘܢ ܘܢܓܕܦܘܢ ܥܠ ܐܠܗܐ ܘܢܐܡܪܘܢ܆ ܡܛܠ
ܕܠܝܬ ܬܘܪܐܝܬ ܕܢܚܙܘܢ ܠܐܠܗܐ. ܡܛܠ ܗܢܐ ܠܝ ܬܘܪ
ܐܕܪ̈ܝܢ ܒܢ̈ܫܬܐ. ܘܒܥܘܪܐ ܕܢܗܘܘܢ ܡܒܕܪ̈ܐ ܒܐܬܪ̈ܘܢ
ܕܡܘܕܝܢ ܒܒܪܐ ܐܚܪܢܐ ܕܦܠܓܐ ܠܗܘܢ. ܠܗܠܝܢ ܗܘ
ܡܪܢ ܡܬܠܐ ܠܗܘܢ ܦܘܢܝܗܘܢ܆ ܐܝܠܝܢ ܕܝܢ ܕܠܐ
ܗܡܢܝܢ ܒܗ ܘܡܬܦܢܝܢ ܒܚ̈ܛܗܐ ܢܬܠܘܢ ܓܦܘܦܐ
ܠܢܘܪܐ. ܘܢܓܐܝܘ ܒܗܘܢ ܘܢܐܡܪܘܢ܆ ܐܦ ܕܝܢ ܗܘܝܢ
ܗܟܢܐ. ܘܐܬܚܫܒ ܠܝ ܐܝܟ ܗܠܝܢ. ܘܐܦ ܗܠܝܢ
ܕܡܗܦܟܝܢ ܒܗܘܢ܆ ܕܒܪܐ ܠܒܝܫܘܢ ܫܒܚܗ ܕܡܪܢ܆
ܒܪܝܘܬܐ ܕܥܠ ܐܢ̈ܫܘܢ ܘܒܕܘܒܪ̈ܐ ܕܒܢܬܐ. ܢܗܘܘܢ
ܫܦ̈ܝܪܐ ܘܡܬ̈ܒܪܢܝܢܐ ܘܗܢ̈ܝܢ ܫ̈ܕܐ. ܙܢܝܢ ܒܗܦܟܐ
ܘܡܬ̈ܦܠܓܢ ܬܘܕ̈ܝܬܐ. ܘܕܠܐ ܢܦܪܫܢ ܦܘܩ̈ܕܢܐ. ܒܪܡ ܩ̈ܠܝܠܐ
ܠܐ ܢܪܫܡܘܢ܆ ܘܒܚܝܠܗܘܢ ܢܬܚܝܠܘܢ ܫ̈ܒܝܚܐ ܐܝܟ
ܐܡܪ̈ܐ ܕܐܬܚܝܠܘܢ ܕܐ̈ܒܐ ܣܓܘ̈ܦܐ. ܘܢܐܟܠܘܢ ||
ܦܘܠܚܢܐ ܕܝ̈ܬܡܐ ܘܢܣܒܘܬܐ ܕܐܪ̈ܡܠܬܐ. ܘܥܠ ܕܢܫܒܩ f. 53 a
ܢܓܠܐ ܕܝܢܐ ܘܢܬܒܥܘܢ ܒܢ̈ܝܗܘܢ ܒܟܘܫܪܐ ܘܢܪܫܥܘܢ
ܫܘܒܗܪܐ. ܘܡܛܠ ܒܚܘܠܡܝܢ ܒܢ̈ܫܬܐ ܕܐܣܬܒܪܘ ܡܢܗܘܢ܆
ܢܛܪܘܢ ܠܡܪܝܐ ܘܠܝܬ ܕܒܥܐ ܠܗܘܢ܆ ܘܠܐ ܢܗܘܐ
ܠܗܘܢ ܦܘܪܩܢܐ. ܡܛܠ ܕܗܦܟ ܒܢ̈ܝܬܐ ܥܠ ܐܪܒܥܐ.
ܘܫܠܘ ܐܦܝ̈ܫܘܗܘܢ ܡܢ ܐܒܐ ܕܒܫܡܝܐ. ܘܢܫܠܡ

ܢܣܒܪܘܢ ܒܫܡܗ ܕܡܪܢ ܝܫܘܥ ܘܠܐ ܢܬܟܦܘܢ܆ ܡܛܠ
ܙܒܘܪܬ ܡܫܝܚܘܬܗܘܢ܆ ܘܩܝܡ ܘܠܐ ܡܫܬܡܥܝܢ. ܡܛܠ
ܕܠܘ ܒܠܚܘܕ ܠܒܢܘܗܝ ܩܐܡ ܠܗ. ܦ̈ܪܫܐ ܕܝܢ ܡܢܗܘܢ
ܙܒܘ̈ܪܝ ܒܡܫܝܚܐ ܫܐܠܝܢ ܘܡܫܬܡܥܝܢ ܡܛܠ ܕܫܪܪܐ
ܡܡܠܠܝܢ ܠܩܘܬܗܘܢ ܘܠܐܠܗܐ ܣܓܕܝܢ. ܘܠܒܪܗ
ܚܒܝܒܐ ܡܫܬܒܚܝܢ. ܘܒܪܘܚܐ ܠܐ ܟܦܪܝܢ. ܘܒܫܡܗܐ
ܙܝܐ ܐܬ̈ܘܬܐ ܘܚܝ̈ܠܐ ܪ̈ܘܪܒܐ ܥܒ̈ܕܝܢ ܘܐܦ ܗܠܝܢ
ܒܡܫܝܚܘܬܗܘܢ ܘܒܡܫܝܚܘܬܐ ܠܐ ܡܫܬܒܩܝܢ ܕܢܐܚܘܢ܆
ܢܦܘܩܘܢ ܠܒܪ ܒܠܝܠܘܢ ܕ̈ܒܢܐ ܕܫܘܪܐ ܘܐܦ ܒܦܘ̈ܪܐ
ܕܫܘܪܐ. ܘܡܛܠ ܫܡܗ ܕܡܪܢ ܢܬܕܒܘܢ܆ ܘܢܬܢܓܕܘܢ܆
ܘܢܬܛܠܠܘܢ ܐܝܟ ܒܡܘ̈ܬܐ ܡ̈ܪܝܪܐ ܘܡ̈ܫܚܠܦܐ. ܘܐܦ
ܡܢ ܒܬܪ ܕܡܬܛܠܠܝܢ ܣܓܝܐܐ ܙܒ̈ܢܐ ܢܣܒܪܘܢ
ܒܡܬܟܬܫܘܬܗܘܢ܆ ܘܡܢ ܒܬܪ ܕܗܠܝܢ ܢܦ̈ܘܩܘܢ. ܬܒܛܠ
ܡܫܝܚܘܬܐ ܡܢ ܐܪܥܐ. ܘܬܬܓܒܪ ܬܪܝܘܬܐ. ܘܐܝܠܝܢ
ܕܡܫܬܡܗܝܢ ܕܒܡܕܝܢ ܒܡܪܢ ܘܡܫܡܕܝܢ ܒܫܡܗ ܗܘܢ
ܢܒܐܫܘܢ ܡܢ ܟܠ ܐܢܫ. ܘܢܬܒܣܘܢ ܒܡܫܝܚܘܬܐ
ܘܢܡܠܠܘܢ ܡܦ̈ܬܠܬܐ ܘܢܓܕܦܘܢܗ܆ ܠܡܪܢ܆ ܘܢܬܚܫܒܘܢ
ܟܡܐ ܙܒܢܐ ܡܠܦ̈ܢܐ ܦ̈ܠܓܢܝܐ. ܟܕ ܪܘܫܗ ܕܐܒܐ ܠܐ
ܡܡܠܠܐ ܒܗܘܢ ܘܢܓܕܦܘܢܗ܆ ܠܡܪܢ܆ ܘܗܕܐ ܟܕ ܗܘ
ܡܠܐ ܒܡܬ̈ܐ ܘܐܒܐ ܕܕܒܪܢܘܬܐ ܘܦܪܢܣܐ. ܗܢܘ ܕܝܢ
ܦܪܢܣܐ. ܢܐܒܕܠ ܒܢܝܢܗܘܢ ܘܢܫܓܘܫ ܪ̈ܚܡܝܢܗܘܢ܆
ܘܢܒܛܠ ܡܫܝܚܘܬܗܘܢ܆ ܘܢܫܘܐ ܕܒܪ ܢܫܡܘܢ
f. 52 b ܘܢܫܬܡܥܘܢ܆ || ܘܢܐܡܪ ܠܟܠܢܫ ܒܐܬܪܗ ܕܐܒܐ ܢܬܐܪܬ
ܕܢܫ ܐܢܫ ܠܐܠܗܐ. ܘܬܬܓܐܬ ܡܕܘܪܐ ܐܢܫܐ.

ܗܘ ܡܫܡܫܢܐ ܐܚܪܢ ܟܠܝܠܗܘܢ: ܘܪܬܝܡܘ ܠܒܘܬܗܘܢ
ܒܪܘܚܐ. ܘܒܫܪܪܐ. ܘܠܐ ܗܘܐ ܠܘܬܗܘܢ: ܘܐܡܪܘ.[1]
ܡܠܠܘ ܡܠܠܘ. ܘܫܪܝܘ ܕܢܫܒܚܘܢ ܘܢܗܠܠܘܢ ܘܢܩܠܣܘܢ
ܘܢܪܡܪܡܘܢ ܠܡܪܢ: ܟܕ [ܫܐ]ܠܝܢ[2] ܗܘܘ ܡܠܝܢ
ܕܬܬܫܡܠܐ ܡܫܡܫܘܬܗ [ܠܘܬܗܘܢ]

ܟܠܝܠܐ ܕܫܡܥܘܢ ܟܐܦܐ

ܘܐܬܬܙܝܚ ܫܡܥܘܢ ܟܪܘܙܐ ܕܐܠܗܐ. ܘܐܬܡܬܚ
ܫܪܗ ܘܦܓܪܐ. ܘܫܒܚܘ ܘܒܟܐ ܘܐܡܪ. ܡܐ ܙܘ̈ܥܝܢ
ܚܕ̈ܝܢ ܡܪܢܐ. ܘܡܠܘܗܝ ܒܫܡܫܬܐ ܒܒܪܬ ܐܢܘܢ:
ܗܐ ܠܒܪ ܣܢܐ ܐܢܐ ܣܠܩܬ̈ܐ ܕܐܠܗܐ. ܕܐܠܦ ܐܠܦܝܢ
ܐܦ ܪ̈ܒܘܬܐ ܕܠܐ ܡܢܝܢ. ܟܕ ܡܝܩܪܝܢ ܒܫܡܝܐ ܘܡܫܒܚܝܢ
ܠܒܪܘܫܐ ܪܒܐ ܕܐܠܗܘܬܐ. ܡܟܠܝܬ ܡܢ ܟܠ. ܘܐܫܬܠܝ
ܠܘܬܝ, ܡܝܟܐܝܠ ܡܠܐܟܐ ܪܒܐ ܕܗܘ ܢܗܘܐ ܠܝ ܡܥܕܪܢܐ.
ܘܡܠܟܬ ܪܘܚܐ ܒܬܝܪܘ. ܘܣܝܡܬ ܠܒܢܝܐ ܕܡܢ ܟܬܪ: ܟܕ
ܡܠܐ ܡܟܫ̈ܘܠܐ. ܘܒܝܫܬܐ ܘܣܘܦ̈ܢܐ ܘܕܓܠܘܬܐ.
ܘܒ̈ܝܫܬܐ ܕܒܗ ܝ̈ܬܒܢܐ ܫ̈ܒܘܫܝܢܐ ܘܡܦ̈ܬܠܬܐ. ܕܠܐܠܗܐ
ܠܐ ܝܕܥܝܢ ܘܠܫܪ̈ܪܐ ܠܐ ܡܫܬܡܥܝܢ. ܘܒܘ̈ܪܐ ܕܝܢ
ܡܠܝܘ ܡܫܬܡܥܝܢ ܠܐܠܗܘܬܐ: ܡܛܠ ܒ̈ܥܕܘܗܝ, ܕܝܕܝܢ
ܒܝܬܗ. ܗܢܝܢ ܕܡܟܝܟܝܢ ܒܪܘܚܐ. ܘܗܢܝܢ ܕܡܟܦ̈ܝܢ
ܒܐܪܥܐ. ܘܐܝܟ ܕܝܕܝܢ ܠܡܪܢ ܐܝܟ ܠܐ ‖ ܝܕܝܢ. f. 52 a
ܫܡܥܐ ܗܘ ܠܡܪܢ ܒܩܠܗ ܦܬܪܐ ܟܠܝܗܘܢ ܕܡܫܡܫܢܐ
ܐܬܚܙܝܘܢ: ܘܢܒܟܘܢ ܡܢ ܒܬܪ ܕܒܢܐ ܕܬܫܡܫܬܐ

[1] We should read ܘܐܡܪ?

[2] MS. illegible.

ܪܒܐ. ܕܠܐ ܚܙܘ ܡܢ ܡܘܕܥܘܗܝ܆ ܐܒܘܬܗ ܒܒܢ̈ܝܐ.
ܘܐܒܘܬܗ ܬܘܒ ܠܐ ܡܨܝܐ ܕܢܗܘܐ ܐܠܐ ܗܘ ܐܝܢܐ
ܕܒܬܪ ܕܢܬܓܠܐ ܒܗ ܡܪܢ܆ ܘܒܬܪ ܗܘ ܢܗܘܪܐ
ܠܟܠܗܘܢ ܫܢ̈ܝܐ ܬܠܬ. ܢܘܡܐ ܗܘܐ ܕܝܢ ܕܒܪܘܒܬܐ.
ܘܠܐ ܒܝܕܐ ܡܫܬܥܒܕ. ܗܘܐ ܡܢ ܓܘ ܢܗܘܪܐ ܕܐܡܪ.
ܒܪܝܟ ܗܘ ܘܡܒܪܟ ܕܐܬܐ ܘܐܬܐ ܒܫܡܗ ܕܡܪܝܐ.
ܡܒܪܟ ܗܘ ܪܐܙܐ ܕܦܘܪܩܢܐ. ܗܟܢܐ ܫܡܥܝܢ ܗܘܘ
ܒܝܡܐ ܕܓܠܠ ܡܢ ܚܠܝܬܐ. ܢܗܘܪܐ ܗܘ. ܘܡܫܝܚܐ ܡܢ
ܫܠܝܐ ܐܝܟܢ ܠܘܬܗܘܢ ܘܠܐ ܘܡܫܡܥܘ ܕܐܡܪ ܦܘܩܘ
ܠܗܘܢ ܠܦܘܪܐ ܠܕܒܘܬܐ ܐܝܕܐ ܕܐܬܚܙܝ܆ ܠܗܘܢ ܒܗ
ܡܘܫܐ ܘܐܠܝܐ. ܘܬܡܢ ܢܬܡܠܠ ܥܡܗܘܢ ܒܪܘܚ:
ܥܠ ܥܠܡܐ ܘܚܪܬܐ. ܘܥܠ ܡܠܟܘܬܐ ܕܐܠܗܐ. ܘܡܠܟܘܢ
ܬܡܠܠܘܗܝ܆ ܠܫܢ̈ܝܐ ܕܐܒܗ̈ܬܐ ܡܢ̈ܝܐ. ܘܟܕ ܫܡܥ
ܗܠܐ. ܢܦܠܝܢ ܗܘܘ ܥܠ ܐܦ̈ܝܗܘܢ ܡܢ ܕܚܠܬܗܘܢ ܦܘܪܐ[1]
ܪܒܐ ܘܦܠܓܐ ܘܒܕ̈ܡܐ ܕܒܢ̈ܝܗܘܢ ܡܫ̈ܢܐ ܡܠܝܐ
ܗܘܬ ܒܠܝܬܐ. ܘܟܕ ܥܡܗܘܢ ܒܐܦܐ ܘܡܚܕܐ
ܚܒܪ̈ܘܗܝ. ܟܕ ܐܬܦܢܝ. ܘܡܬܕܟܝܢ ܒܪܘܚܐ ܕܩܘܕܫܐ.
ܘܐܙܠ ܠܐܬܪܐ ܕܘܡܒܕ[2] ܐܘܢ ܢܣܒ. ܘܗܘܘ ܬܡܢ
f. 51b ܒܗ ܝܕܥܝܢ ܘܡܫܠܡܝܢ ܡܩ̈ܕܝܢ ܥܕ̈ܡܐ. ܘܡܦܩܝܢ || [ܠܗ
ܐܒ]ܠܘ[3] ܘܡܢ[4] ܥܠܝܐ ܐܬܬܦܫܡܘ ܗܘܘ [ܦܬܘܪ̈ܐ][3]
ܡܕܡܝܘܗܝ ܟܕ ܡܠܝܢ ܥܠ ܦܘܬ̈ܝܢ ܡܕܝܢ̈ܬܐ [ܘܡܢ
ܐܢܚܒܐ][3] ܐܬܚܙܝܘܗܝ ܡܪܢ ܟܕ ܚܙܘܗ. ܡܢ ܡܚܐ
ܕܗܘ ܐܫܬܕܪ. ܘܠܦܪܘܗܝ ܕܢܡܘܣܐ ܐܒܘܬܗ [ܕܢܡܘܣ]ܐ

¹ Second hand (?) adds the vowel ܳ over ܦ ² Cod. ܕܘܡܒ

³ MS. torn ⁴ The second hand suggests ܐܫܬܕܪ ܠܗܘܢ ܡܢ

 ||

¹ Cod.   ² Better

ܡܠܘ ܝܗܒ ܠܗܘܢ ܗܕܐ ܘܐܝܟܢܐ ܐܬܪܝܘ. ܕܗܘܐ ܫܡܥܝܢ ܕܡܫܡܠܝܢ ܒܫ̈ܢܝܐ ܫ̈ܪܬܐ ܕܠܐ ܐܠܝܨܝܢ[1] ܒܗܘܢ܁ ܘܡܚܪܝܢ ܬܝܒܘܬܐ ܘܡܬܚܠܝܢ ܒܒ̈ܢܝܢܫܐ ܠܡܠܟܘܬܐ ܕܐܠܗܐ. ܠܐ ܗܘܐ ܒܝܬ ܐܬܠܝܕܘ ܘܒܩܡ ܪܒܘ. ܘܡܫ̈ܝܚܐ ܒܐܝ̈ܕܝܬܐ ܐܬܝܗܒܘܢ ܗܘܘ. ܘܗܢܐ ܫܡܥܝܢ ܡܢܗܘܢ ܒܡ̈ܬܐ ܘܓܠ̈ܝܬܐ ܐܝܠܝܢ ܕܠܥܒܐ[2] ܕܒ̈ܢܝܢܫܐ ܠܐ ܡܨܐ ܕܢܡܠܠ ܐܢܫ܁ ܗܕܐ ܓܝܪ ܠܝܬܗ̇ ܒܠܒܪ ܡܢ ܓܒܝܐ ܕܐܠܗܐ. ܗܝ ܕܒܬܪܗ̇ ܠܗܠܝܢ.

ܡܢ ܒܬܪ ܕܝܢ ܕܡܠܦܝܢ ܗܘܘ ܘܡܚܪܬܝܢ ܠܒܢܝܐ ܐܝܟ ܕܐܬܦܩܕܘ ܡܢ ܡܪܢ܁ ܐܬܒܢܝܘ[3] ܠܒܠܝܬܐ ܗܝ ܕܗܘܝܢ ܗܘܘ ܒܗ̇ ܒܗ ܢܦܫ ܘܦܓܪܘ ܘܪܘܚܗ ܠܐܠܗܐ. ܘܒܟܠ ܒܠܗܘܢ ܐܝܟ ܕܚܙܝܐ ܢܦܫ[4]. ܕܢܫܬܡܠܐ ܒܠܚܕ ܡܢܗܘܢ ܒܠܒܝܐ ܕܚܒܪܗ ܘܕܡܫܡܠܝܢ. ܘܡܢ ܒܬܪܟ ܒܚܕܐ ܫܘܝܘܬܐ ܘܐܘܝܘܬܐ ܢܫܐܠܘܢ ܡܢ ܐܠܗܐ ܡܗܡܢܘܬܐ ܗܝ ܕܐܫܬܘܕܝ ܠܗܘܢ܁ ܘܢܛܠܒܐ ܠܗܘܢ ܒܠ ܚܪܬܐ. ܘܦܪܩܘ ܫܡܥܘܢ ܒܐܦܐ ܘܢܚܪܒܘܪ ܬܠܡ̈ܝܕܐ ܘܦܩܕ ܐܠܗܐ ܒܗ̇ ܒܒܠܝܬܐ ܘܓܠܝܘ ܘܒܟܘ ܡܢ ܐܠܗܐ ܘܐܡܪܘ.

ܨܠܘܬܐ ܗܕܐ

f. 50 b ܡܪܝܐ ܐܠܗܐ ܫܠܝܛܐ ܐܒܘܗܝ، ܘܫܠܝܚܗ ‖ ܕܡܪܢ ܝܫܘܥ ܡܫܝܚܐ. ܗܘ ܕܫܪܪܬܝܗܝ، ܠܒܪܟ ܝܚܝܕܝܐ ܕܢܚܙܪ ܠܝ ܡܢ ܒܝܫܐ: ܘܡܢ ܛܘܥܝܝ. ܘܢܕܪܐ ܒܐܘܪܚܐ ܕܚܝ̈ܐ.

[1] Second hand ܐܠܝܨܝܢ [2] Cod. ܕܠܥ̈ܒܐ [3] First hand omits.

[4] Cod. ܢܦܫ

ܘܐܬܡܠܠܘܢ ܒܠܫ̈ܢܐ ܡܫܚܠܦܐ. ܘܡܕܡ ܠܗ ܢܬܒܥܐ
ܡܡܠܠܘܢ؛ ܘܪܘܚ ܩܘܕܫܐ ܗܘܬ ܒܗܘܢ؛ ܘܕܝܪܝܢ، ܘܡܕܝܢܬ
ܒܡܬ̈ܒܘܢ؛ ܠܝܗܘܕܝܐ ܘܠܓܝܘܪܐ ܘܠܚܢܦܐ ܕܡܠܟܘܬܐ
ܕܫܡܝܐ. ܕܐܝܠܝܢ ܕܗܘܝܢ ܘܫܡܥܝܢ ܘܗܦܟܝܢ ܠܬ̈ܠܡܝܕܘܢ؛
ܠܐ ܗܘܐ ܐܝܟ ܡܗܦܟ̈ܢܐ ܐܫ̈ܬܢܐ ܕܡܡܠܠܝܢ ܡܕܡ
ܕܫܡܥܘ. ܘܡܬܡܗܝܢ ܡܕܡ ܕܫܡܥܘ. ܐܢܬܘܢ ܕܝܢ ܒܪܘܚܗ
ܕܐܒܝ ܬܡܠܠܘܢ؛ ܠܗܠܝܢ ܕܫܡܥܝܢ ܘܠܗܠܝܢ ܕܟܬ̈ܒܝܢ؛
ܘܐܠܝܢ ܕܡܫܡܫܝܢ ܘܗܦܟܝܢ ܚܙܘܢ ܚܙ̈ܘܐ ܚܕ̈ܬܐ.
ܒܡܠܟܘܬܐ ܕܐܒܝ ܕܒܫܡܝܐ.

ܘܡܫܝܕܐ ܐܬܒܥܝ ܡܪܢ ܡܢ ܬܪ̈ܥܝܬܗ. ܘܪܘܚܐ
ܕ̈ܒܢܝܗܘܢ[1] ܐܝܟ ܢܘܪܐ ܕܝܩܕܐ. ܘܐܬܦܫܛ ܠܟܠܚܕ ܚܕ
ܡܢܗܘܢ ܠܫܢܐ ܘܦܠܓܘܬܐ ܘܡܠܠ ܒܗܘܢ ܫܡܥܘܢ
ܒܟܪܝܐܝܬ. ܘܝܥܩܘܒ ܪܗܘܡܐܝܬ. ܘܝܘܚܢ ܢܒܝܐܝܬ.
ܘܐܢܕܪܐܘܣ ܦܠܫܬܐܝܬ. ܘܦܝܠܝܦܘܣ ܐܓܦܛܐܝܬ.
ܘܒܪ ܬܘܠܡܝ ܐܠܢܐܝܬ[2] ܘܡܬܝ، ܦܪܬܐܝܬ. ܘܬܘܡܐ
ܗܢܕܘܐܝܬ. ܘܝܥܩܘܒ ܒܪ ܚܠܦܝ ܒܠܫܢܐ ܕܒܝܬ ܢܗܪܝܢ.
ܕܒܒܝܪ ܢܗܪܐ. ܘܬܐܕܝ، ܦܪܣܐܝܬ. ܘܫܡܥܘܢ ܩܢܢܝܐ
ܡܕܝܐܝܬ. ܘܡܬܝܐ ܒܠܫܢܐ ܕܦܪܣ. ܗܠܘܢ ܕܝܢ ܗܘܘ
ܡܕܡ || ܕܡܡܠܠܝܢ ܒܠܫܢ ܠܫܢܐ ܕܥܡܪܗ. ܘܗܘܘ[3] ܟܠܗܘܢ f. 50 a
ܐܠܝܢ ܕܫܡܥܝܢ ܗܘܘ ܠܗܘܢ ܡܬܕܡܪܝܢ ܗܘܘ ܘܡܫܬܟܚܝܢ.
ܘܐܡܪܝܢ ܗܘܘ. ܕܐܝܟܢܐ ܗܠܝܢ ܒܢܝ̈ܢܫܐ ܘܡܚ̈ܠܦܐ ܡܢ
ܥܠ ܗܘܘ ܫܟܝܪܐ. ܘܡ̈ܠܟܠ ܡܫܡܫܬܐ ܦܠܓܝܢ ܒܫ̈ܦܬܐ.

[1] Second hand adds ܘܐܬܒܠܥܘ [2] As in Acts ii. 9.

[3] Query ܘܗܘܐ?

ܡܢ ܕܕܝܢܟ. ܘܐܬܚܫܒ ܠܟ ܥܠ ܫܘܠܛܢ ܕܒܫܡܝܐ
ܘܒܐܪܥܐ. ܘܦܩܕܬ ܠܢ ܕܬܠܡܝܕܐ ܫ̈ܕܬܐ ܢܕܒܪ:

ܘܡܢ ܒܬܪܟܢ ܨܠܘܬܐ ܗܕܐ ܘܐܡܪܘ[1]

ܒܥܘ ܡܢܟ ܡܪܢ ܘܐܠܗܢ ܠܐ ܬܫܒܘܩ ܡܢܢ
ܦܘܩܕܢܟ. ܐܠܐ ܫܪܪ ܠܢ ܒܦܘܩܕܢܟ ܘܐܟܬܪ ܠܢ
ܒܐܝܕܥܬܐ ܕܡܢܟ. ܘܥܡ ܠܢ ܪܘܚܟ ܩܕܝܫܐ. ܘܗܒ ܠܢ
ܪ̈ܚܡܐ ܘܚܝܠܐ ܕܡܢܟ. ܘܫܡܠܐ ܥܡܢ ܡܗܝܡܢܘܬܐ ܕܡܢܟ.
ܘܥܡ ܐܝܠܝܢ ܕܩܪܝܢ ܒܫܡܟ ܫܪܝܪܐܝܬ ܠܐ ܬܬܥܪܒ
ܠܘܬܢ ܦܘܪܫܢ. ܘܠܐ ܢܦܩ ܠܢ ܐܒܠܘܢܝܐ ܒܐܘܪ̈ܚܬܗ
ܡܘܢܕ̈ܝܐ. ܘܠܐ ܢܠܟܢ ܡܢ ܡܪܬܐ ܕܥܘܠܐ ܚܡܝܡܐ.
ܕܗܘ ܗܘܐ ܥܠܬܐ ܕܡܦܘܠܬܐ ܠܐܒܘܢ ܐܕܡ. ܐܠܐ
ܗܘܝ ܠܢ ܐܝܟ ܪܥܝܐ ܘܡܢܘܚܐ. ܘܡܪܐ ܘܡܕܒܪܢܐ
ܘܡܦܝܣܢܐ ܘܡܫܘܙܒܢܐ. ܘܟܠ ܡܐ ܕܡܢܟ ܡܬܚܫܒ ܠܢ.
ܒܥܘܠ ܦܘܩܕܢܟ ܢܫܬܡܠܐ ܒܢܢ. ܫܕܪܐ ܠܫܘܠܛܢܗ
ܕܥܠܡܐ. ܐܘ ܡܪܢ ܐܟܬܪ ܠܢ ܐܝܟ ܫܘ̈ܕܝܢܟ.
ܕܢܡܠܠ ܒܠܫ̈ܢܐ ܚܕ̈ܬܐ. ܒܪܘܚܐ ܕܡܢܟ. ܘܢܣܒ[2] ܡܢܐ
ܗܝ ܚܕܬܐ ܕܥܠܡܐ. ܡܛܠ ܕܒܢܝܬ ܒܥ̈ܠܝܐ ܘܡܫܘ̈ܥܠܐ
ܕܥܠܡܐ ܡܢܟܝܢ. ܟܠܗ ܦܫܩ ܠܢ ܡܪܢ ܐܡܒܢܐ ܗܝ
ܡܫܬܬܟ. ܘܡܪܢܐ ܗܝ ܣܐܪܬܐ[3]. ܘܡܪܢܐ ܡܡܥ̈ܠܝܐ
ܡܢܝܢ ܒܥܠܡܐ. ܕܗܐ ܡܫܬܥܠܐ ܐܢܬ ܡܢܢ. ܘܡܪܢܐ ||
f. 49 b ܢܐܡܪ ܠܐ ܕܒܢܝܢ. ܘܒܐܐ ܒܗܘܢ ܢܣܒ ܘܐܡܪ
ܠܡܪܢܐ ܗܢܐ ܒܠܗ ܕܒܪܢܝܐ ܗܝܡܢܘܬܗܘܢ: ܗܐ
ܝܗܒܬ ܠܟܘܢ ܫܘܒܩܢ ܘܫܠܡܘܬ ܠܬܘܒܢ ܫܠ̈ܝܚܘܬܗܘܢ:

[1] Cod. ܘܐܡܪ [2] Cod. ܘܣܒ [3] Read ܚܪܬܐ

 f. 49 a
---

¹ The MS. is torn at the edge and the last letter almost illegible.
I do not think it is   ² The second hand adds on the margin
          ³ Cod.

ܘܐܢܕܪܐܘܣ ܘܐܚܘܗܝ، ܡܢ ܫܒܛܐ ܕܙܒܘܠܘܢ؛ ܘܦܝܠܝܦܘܣ ܡܢ ܫܒܛܐ ܕܝܘܣܦ. ܘܒܪ ܬܘܠܡܝ ܡܢ ܫܒܛܐ ܕܝܣܫܟܪ؛ ܘܡܬܝ، ܡܢ ܫܒܛܐ ܕܢܦܬܠܝ. ܘܬܐܘܡܐ ܡܢ ܫܒܛܐ ܕܒܢܝܡܝܢ. ܘܝܥܩܘܒ ܒܪ ܚܠܦܝ ܡܢ ܫܒܛܐ ܕܠܘܝ. ܘܬܕܝ، ܡܢ ܫܒܛܐ ܕܝܗܘܕܐ. ܘܫܡܥܘܢ ܩܢܢܝܐ ܡܢ ܫܒܛܐ ܕܐܫܝܪ. ܘܝܗܘܕܐ ܗܘ ܕܐܫܠܡܗ ܡܢ ܫܒܛܐ ܕܓܕ ∴ ܬܪ̈ܥܣܪ ܗܠܝܢ ܬܠܡܝ̈ܕܘܗܝ، ܕܡܠܟ ܠܗܘܢ ܬܪ̈ܥܣܪ ܟܘܪ̈ܣܘܬܐ. ܕܗܘܢ ܢܕܘܢ ܠܐܝܣܪܝܠ. ܘܗܘܐ ܟܕ ܡܪܢ[1] ܣܥܪ ܗܠܝܢ ܟܠܗܘܢ ܬܕܡܪ̈ܬܐ. ܘܡܠܦ ܒܟܢܘܫ̈ܬܐ. ܘܒܡ̈ܕܝܢܬܐ ܘܒܫܘ̈ܩܐ ܡܠܬܐ ܕܐܠܗܐ. ܘܐܬܐܒܫ ܪ̈ܒܝ ܟܗ̈ܢܐ ܘܣܦܪ̈ܐ ܕܥܡܐ. ܘܡܬܚܣܡܝܢ ܗܘܘ ܥܠܘܗܝ، ܠܪ̈ܫܢܐ ܘܠܩܫܝ̈ܫܐ، ܫܘܠܛܢܐ. ܒܥܡܐ ܕܐܬܚܘ ܥܠܘܗܝ، ܒܠܠܝ̈ܬܐ ܘܣܗܕܘ̈ܬܐ ܟܕ ܫܡܥܘܢ ܐܝܟܢܐ ܕܢܣܒܪܘܢܝܗܝ، ܐܝܟ ܕܡܬܟܬܒܐ ܒܠܗ̇ ܡܣܒܪܢܘܬܐ ܒܐܘܢܓܠܝܘܢ ܘܕܝܢܐ ܕܐܪ̈ܒܥܐ ܡܣܒܪ̈ܢܐ ܫܪܝܪ̈ܐ. ܘܟܡܐ ܐܢܘܢ ܡܟܪ؛ ܘܐܡܪ ܠܗܘܢ؛ ܕܗܘܝܢ ܢܦܩܘܢ ܢܣܒܪܘܢ ܒܐܪ̈ܒܥ ܦܢܝ̈ܬܐ ܕܒܪܝܬܐ. ܘܢܩܦܘܢ ܒܪ̈ܘܬܐ ܗܐ ܡܢ ܣܘܦܝܗ̇ ܕܐܪܥܐ ܥܕܡܐ ܠܣܘܦܝܗ̇.

ܒܬܪܟܢ ܕܝܢ ܕܥܒܕܘ[2] ܟܠܗܘܢ، ܢܟܠܐ ܡܫܘ̈ܕܥܐ. ܬܪ̈ܥ ܟܗ̈ܢܐ ܘܣܦܪ̈ܐ ܕܥܡܐ ܒܝܕ ܚܕ ܡܢ ܬܠܡܝ̈ܕܘܗܝ، f. 48 b ܐܝܢܐ ܕܫܡܗ ܣܟܪܝܘܛܐ ‖ ܘܫܠܡ ܟܣܦܐ ܠܦܘܩܕܢܗܘܢ. ܘܐܫܠܡܗ ܠܗܘܢ؛ ܘܗܢܘܢ ܐܫܠܡܘܗܝ، ܠܕܝ̈ܢܐ ܘܕܢܘܗܝ. ܘܨܠܒܘܗܝ، ܘܡܝܬ. ܘܐܬܩܒܪ ܘܩܡ ܠܬܠܬܐ ܝܘ̈ܡܝܢ

[1] Cod. ܡܪܢ ܟܕ   [2] Cod. ܥܒܕ

ܘܒܪܬܗ ܡܪܝܡ ܘܐܘܕܝܬ ܠܐܠܗܐ ܘܐܡܪܬ. ܡܪܝ،
ܢܗܘܐ ܠܝ ܐܝܟ ܡܠܬܟ. ܘܝܠܕܬ ܡܪܝܡ ܒܒܝܬ ܠܚܡ
ܕܝܗܘܕܐ. ܘܐܫܬܡܥ ܠܗ ܫܡܥܐ ܫܘܒ. ܦܪܘܣܐ ܘܡܠܟܐ.
ܘܐܠܗܐ ܕܟܠ ܟܠ. ܐܝܟ ܕܐܡܪ ܪܘܚܐ ܩܕܝܫܐ.
ܒܦܘܡܗ ܕܕܘܝܕ ܢܒܝܐ. ܘܡܠܟܝܕܡ ܗܘ ܬܫܡܫ ܙ̈ܟܠܘܗܝ.
ܚܙܐ ܘܒܣ̈ܪܐ ܟܠܗܘܢ. ܐܦ ܚܝܘܬܐ ܕܕܒܪܐ ܘܦ̈ܪܐ
ܕܒܡܕܒܪܐ. ܩ̈ܠܠܐ ܕܫܡܝܐ ܕܒܟܝܢ ܒܫܒ̈ܝܠܐ ܕܫܡ̈ܝܐ.
ܘܐܫܬܒܩ ܠܗ ܠܥܡܐ ܫܘܒ. ܟܠ ܕܒܡܕܒܪܐ ܘܟܠ
ܕܒܐܪܥܐ. ܘܡܢ ܒܬܪ ܙܒܢܐ ܩܠܝܠ ܕܫ̈ܢܝܐ ܬܩ̈ܢܝܐ.
ܒܪܝ ܡܢ ܚܘܪܒܗ ܠܡܬܘܪܢ. ܕܐܬܟܠܐ ܟܠ ܕܩ̈ܬܝܢ.
ܘܡܢ ܒܬܪ ܡܘܬܗ ܕܗܘܪܘܕܣ ܐܬܓܠܝ ܡܠܐܟܐ ܠܝ
ܝܘܣܦ. ܘܐܗܦܟܗ ܠܛܠܝܐ ܠܐܪܥܐ ܕܐܝܣܪܐܝܠ. ܘܪܒܐ
ܗܘܐ ܘܡܫܬܡܠܐ ܒܥܘܡܪܬܐ ܐܝܟ ܕܟܬܝܒ ܒܐܘܪ̈ܝܬܐ
ܕܢܒ̈ܝܐ ܫܪ̈ܝܪܐ ܘܟܪܘܙܘܬܐ ܗܝ ܕܐܘܢܓܠܝܘܢ ܩܕܝܫܐ.
ܘܗܟܢ ܗܘܐ ܒܟܠܗܝܢ ܚܝܠܐ ܪ̈ܘܪܒܐ ܘܬܕܡ̈ܪܬܐ
ܡܫܬ̈ܡܥܬܐ ܕܠܐ ܡܢܝܢ. ܐܝܠܝܢ ܕܗܘ̈ܟܐ ܡܟܬܒܢ
ܥܡ ܡܟܪ̈ܙܢܐ ܕܐܘܢܓܠܝܘܢ ܩܕܝܫܐ. ܒܪ̈ܫܐ ܡܐܗܐ
ܗܘܐ. ܘܦ̈ܪܚܐ ܡܬܒܥܐ ܗܘܐ. ܡܢ̈ܬܐ ܡܫܡܫ ܗܘܐ.
ܚ̈ܡܪܐ ܡܦܬܚ ܗܘܐ. ܡܥܪ̈ܒܐ ܡܫܠ ܗܘܐ. ܒܩ̈ܪܐ
ܡܚܒܒ ܗܘܐ. ܘܐܬ̈ܘܬܐ ܚܒܪ ܗܘܐ. ܘܦ̈ܓܪܐ ܠܗ
ܬܠܡ̈ܝܕܐ ܫܪ̈ܝܐ ܘܫܠ̈ܝܚܐ ܬܪ̈ܥܝܢ. ܕܢܗܘܘܢ || ܒܟܡܗ. f. 48 a
ܕܐܬܚܙܝܘܗܝ ܫܡܥܘܢ ܗܠܝܢ. ܫܡܥܘܢ ܕܐܬܩܪܝ
ܟܐܦܐ. ܘܐܬܚܙܝܘܗܝ ܡܢ ܫܡܝܐ ܕܐܘܪܫܠܡ. ܘܝܥܩܘܒ
ܘܝܘܚܢܢ ܒܢ̈ܝ ܙܒܕܝ. ܘܐܬܚܙܝܘܗܝ ܡܢ ܫܡܝܐ ܕܐܝܣܛܪ.

f. 47 a ܐܘܣܛܠܘܢ ܕܐܬܪܟܘܪ ܬܠܝܬܝܐ ܡܕ̈ܝܢܬܐ. ܘܟܠܝܘܗܝ
ܕܟܠܫ ܚܕ ܡܢܗܘܢ: ܕܢܦܩ ܡܢ ܒܒܪܐ ܠܒܘܫܐ:
ܘܡܢ ܢܘܚܐ ܠܦܘܪܩܢܐ:

ܦܪܫܐ ܕܐܘܣܛܠܘܢ ܕܫܘܒ ܡܫܝܚܐ. ܒܪܗ ܕܐܠܗܐ
ܚܝܐ. ܐܝܟ ܕܐܡܪ ܒܪܘܚܐ ܕܩܘܕܫܐ ܕܡܫܪܪ ܡܠܐܟܐ
ܡܕܡ ܦܪ̈ܘܩܗ ܕܢܬܠܡ ܐܘܪܚܐ ܕܠܗ ⁘

ܗܘܐ ܕܝܢ ܒܫܢܬ ܬܠܬܡ̈ܐܐ ܘܬܫܥ ܕܐܠܟܣܢܕܪܘܣ
ܒܪ ܦܝܠܝܦܘܣ ܡܩܕܘܢܝܐ ܒܡܠܟܘܬܗ ܕܛܝܒܪܝܘܣ ܩܣܪ:
ܒܪܝܫܢܘܬܐ ܕܗܪܘܕܝܣ ܡܕܒܪܢܐ ܕܝ̈ܗܘܕܝܐ. ܢܚܬ
ܓܒܪܐܝܠ ܡܠܐܟܐ ܪܫ ܡܠܐ̈ܟܐ ܒܣܘܥܪܢܐ ܕܐܠܗܐ
ܠܢܨܪܬ. ܠܘܬ ܒܬܘܠܬܐ ܕܡܬܡܟܪܐ ܡܪܝܡ ܡܢ ܝܘܣܦ
ܕܝܗܘܕܐ. ܒܪ ܐܝܣܪܐܝܠ ܐܝܕܐ ܕܡܟܝܪܐ ܗܘܬ ܠܝܘܣܦ.
ܒܐܝܕܐ. ܘܐܬܚܙܝ ܠܗ̇ ܘܐܡܪ ܕܗܐ ܕܢܚ ܡܢܟܝ ܗܘ
ܕܡܠܟ ܥܡ ܐܒܗ̈ܬܗ: ܘܢܗܘܐ ܦܪܘܩܐ ܠܐܝܣܪܐܝܠ:
ܘܢܗܘܘܢ ܐܝܠܝܢ ܕܠܐ ܡܗܝܡܢ ܒܗ ܢܐܒܕܘܢ: ܡܛܠ
ܕܫܘܠܛܢܗ ܒܫܪܘܪܐ ܒܠܒܐ. ܘܡܠܟܘܬܗ ܠܐ ܒܒܪܐ.
ܗܕܝܢ ܡܪܝܡ ܐܬܬܙܝܥܬ ܡܢ ܡܠܬܐ ܗܕܐ. ܘܐܬܪܗܒܬ
ܠܒ. ܘܦܢܝܬ ܡܪܝܡ ܘܐܡܪܬ. ܘܐܝܟܢܐ ܐܝܟ ܕܐܡܪܬ
ܡܫܟܚܐ ܗܕܐ ܕܬܗܘܐ. ܕܠܝ ܓܒܪܐ ܠܐ ܚܟܝܡ ܠܝ.
ܘܠܕܐ ܡܫܒܪܬ ܠܝ. ܘܐܡܪ ܠܗ̇ ܡܠܐܟܐ. ܫܪܪܐܝܬ
f. 47 b ܡܛܠ ܕܐܠܗܐ ܕܪܒܘܬܐ ܓܒܐ. || ܡܢ ܒܕܘ ܪܘܚܐ ܡܕܝܫܐ
ܐܬܬܐ. ܘܡܪܝܐ ܫܪܐ ܒܟܝ.